THE IMPORTANCE OF

Margaret Mead

by
Rafael Tilton

Lucent Books, P.O. Box 289011, San Diego, CA 92198-9011

These and other titles are included in The Importance Of biography series:

Cleopatra	Margaret Mead
Christopher Columbus	Michelangelo
Marie Curie	Wolfgang Amadeus Mozart
Thomas Edison	Napoleon
Albert Einstein	Richard M. Nixon
Benjamin Franklin	Jackie Robinson
Galileo Galilei	Anwar Sadat
Thomas Jefferson	Margaret Sanger
Chief Joseph	Mark Twain
Malcolm X	H.G. Wells

Library of Congress Cataloging-in-Publication Data

Tilton, Rafael.
    Margaret Mead / by Rafael Tilton.
    p. cm.—(Importance of)
    Includes bibliographical references and index.
Summary: A biography of the woman whose studies of primitive cultures established her as one of the world's most acclaimed anthropologists.
    ISBN 1-56006-039-5 (acid free paper)
    1. Mead, Margaret, 1901-1978—Juvenile literature.
2. Anthropologist—United States—Biography—Juvenile literature. 3. Ethnology—Melanesia—Juvenile literature.
4. Melanesia—Social life and customs—Juvenile literature.
[1. Mead, Margaret, 1901-1978. 2. Anthropologists.] I.Title.
II. Series.
GN21.M36T56   1994
301'.092—dc20   93-21840
[B]   CIP
                                                         AC

Contents

Foreword

THE IMPORTANCE OF biography series deals with individuals who have made a unique contribution to history. The editors of the series have deliberately chosen to cast a wide net and include people from all fields of endeavor. Individuals from politics, music, art, literature, philosophy, science, sports, and religion are all represented. In addition, the editors did not restrict the series to individuals whose accomplishments have helped change the course of history. Of necessity, this criterion would have eliminated many whose contribution was great, though limited. Charles Darwin, for example, was responsible for radically altering the scientific view of the natural history of the world. His achievements continue to impact the study of science today. Others, such as Chief Joseph of the Nez Percé, played a pivotal role in the history of their own people. While Joseph's influence does not extend much beyond the Nez Percé, his nonviolent resistance to white expansion and his continuing role in protecting his tribe and his homeland remain an inspiration to all.

These biographies are more than factual chronicles. Each volume attempts to emphasize an individual's contributions both in his or her own time and for posterity. For example, the voyages of Christopher Columbus opened the way to European colonization of the New World. Unquestionably, his encounter with the New World brought monumental changes to both Europe and the Americas in his day. Today, however, the broader impact of Columbus's voyages is being critically scrutinized. *Christopher Columbus,* as well as every biography in The Importance Of series, includes and evaluates the most recent scholarship available on each subject.

Each author includes a wide variety of primary and secondary source quotations to document and substantiate his or her work. All quotes are footnoted to show readers exactly how and where biographers derive their information, as well as provide stepping stones to further research. These quotations enliven the text by giving readers eyewitness views of the life and times of each individual covered in The Importance Of series.

Finally, each volume is enhanced by photographs, bibliographies, chronologies, and comprehensive indexes. For both the casual reader and the student engaged in research, The Importance Of biographies will be a fascinating adventure into the lives of people who have helped shape humanity's past, present, and will continue to shape its future.

Important Dates in the Life of Margaret Mead

Born in Philadelphia. — **1901**

Chooses career in anthropology; marries Luther Cressman.

Gets curator position at AMNH; makes field trip to Samoa.

1923

1925

Divorces Luther; marries Reo; field trip to Manus with Reo; *Coming of Age in Samoa* is published.

1928

Growing Up in New Guinea published. — **1930**

1931-1933 — Field trip to New Guinea.

Writes *Sex and Temperament*; starts work with Larry Frank.

1935

1935-

Divorces Reo; marries Bateson; field trip to Bali/Iatmul.

Daughter Mary Catherine Bateson born.

1937

1939

Balinese Character published; writes *And Keep Your Powder Dry;* begins wartime work; gives speeches in Britain, U.S.; appointed Executive Secretary of Food Habits Committee.

Begins work with United Nations; organizes *Culture at a Distance.*

1942

1945

1949

Takes Catherine to Australia. — **1952**

Male and Female is published; divorces Bateson.

1953

New Lives for Old published. — **1955**

Restudy of Manus.

Family published with K. Heyman.

1956

1957

Catherine stays in Israel.

1961 — Starts writing for *Redbook.*

Awarded Pulitzer prize; Catherine's daughter born; retires from AMNH.

1969

Hall of the Peoples of the Pacific dedicated to Mead; publishes *Rap on Race* with James Baldwin.

1970

Awarded UNESCO Kalingo Prize for popularization of science.

1971

1975 — Publishes *World Enough.*

Dies of cancer. — **1978**

Setting Out to Change the World

During the years of Margaret Mead's life, from 1901 to 1978, the world changed drastically, and Mead participated fully in these changes. In her pioneering work as an anthropologist, Mead was part of a revolution that changed the roles of men and women in society. A strong woman with an important career, she provided an example of the potential that all women can attain. And in her studies, Mead wrote about the limitations of male/female roles and the need for people to live full, rich lives unbounded by society's cultural restrictions.

In her pursuit of her work, Mead seemed to fear nothing. In a time when women were expected to raise children and tend their homes, she tromped through the Pacific Islands, studying foreign cultures and attempting to make them understandable to an untutored audience. For Mead was not content to be an intellectual whose studies had no effect on her own culture. Instead, she believed that everything she worked for needed to be communicated to a larger public. Her goals were grand—world peace, multicultural understanding, and help for children everywhere. She worked toward these goals diligently and knew that she could only attain them by making people everywhere understand and work toward those same ends.

Today, many of the issues to which Mead devoted her life remain important. She wrote hundreds of articles and over forty books that discussed marriage, education, child-rearing, prejudice, and international issues such as world health and cooperation. And, although some of her work and methodology has been questioned, she is remembered as an undaunted, and tireless figure striving to understand people—and help others to understand them.

Margaret Mead devoted her life to helping children of all cultures and promoting multicultural understanding and world peace.

1 An Unconventional Childhood

Margaret Mead grew up in a busy, unconventional household that was constantly on the move. "For me," she said in her autobiography, *Blackberry Winter*, "moving and staying at home, traveling and arriving, are all of a piece. The world is full of homes."[1] In fact, Margaret lived in at least sixty houses by the time she was thirteen. Most of these temporary homes were in small towns near Philadelphia, Pennsylvania, where Margaret was born on December 16, 1901.

From an early age Margaret was undaunted by this "refugee" life. She explored every part of each new home and neighborhood, finding out which other children lived nearby, and whether there were wildflowers, woods, or hidden areas that could be shaped into imaginary worlds of jungle or primeval forest.

Margaret lived with her parents, her brother and sisters, and her father's mother, Martha Adaline (Ramsey) Mead. Margaret's brother, Richard, was born when Margaret was a year and a half old; in the following seven years, three sisters were born, one of whom died in infancy.

Margaret's grandmother had come to live with her son and daughter-in-law shortly after the two married. A pioneering woman, Martha Mead had been a teacher in her hometown of Winchester, Ohio. At the time of her husband's death, when her son Edward was six years old, Martha had been promoted to the position of principal in the school where her husband had been superintendent. Her

Martha Mead, Margaret's grandmother, had a career in a time when it was highly unusual for women to work outside the home.

career was highly unusual for a woman during the late 1800s, and it set a standard for the next three generations of women in the Mead family.

Her grandmother played a large role in Margaret's early learning. Throughout the family's many moves, she directed Margaret's education, training her in reading, literature, geography, ecology, and botany. Margaret later remembered her grandmother as living "at the center of our household, . . . the place to which we immediately went when we came in from playing or home from school."[2]

"It was my grandmother who gave me my ease in being a woman," Margaret recalled in *Blackberry Winter*.

> She was unquestionably feminine— small and dainty and pretty and wholly without masculine protest or feminist aggrievement. She had gone to college when this was a very unusual thing for a girl to do, she had a firm grasp of anything she paid attention to, she had married and had a child, and she had a career of her own.[3]

Margaret's mother, Emily Fogg, also contributed to Margaret's early values and attitudes toward a woman's role. Emily, like her mother-in-law, had a career of her own. In fact, it was Emily's sociology thesis that caused the Mead family's spring and fall moves to Hammonton, New Jersey. In Hammonton, Emily could interview Italian families who had recently settled in the United States during the great immigration of the early 1900s. In addition, Emily was active in groups that sought better wages for telephone operators, most of whom were women. Margaret recalled that her mother was "filled with passionate resentment about the condition of women."[4]

Margaret's mother, Emily Fogg, with Margaret as a child. Emily was a career woman who often spoke out on the living conditions of poor women.

She also had a sense of justice that, for example, made her refuse to wear the fashionable hats of the time, which were decorated with egret plumes, because she did not approve of killing wild creatures for their furs and feathers. Emily's devoted attention to her studies and her causes left Margaret with a strong impression that women were active participants in the world.

Margaret's father, Edward Mead, had studied economics and worked as a professor at the University of Pennsylvania. He was often away from home in the years after the Depression, because he felt that he was not making a large enough salary. This dissatisfaction led him to seek out and participate in many shaky business ventures, some of which Margaret recalls

Edward Mead's preoccupation with work often kept him from his family. Margaret missed her father's company and attention.

The Older Sister

As the eldest child, Margaret took on a lot of responsibility in this busy family. In her autobiography, she recalls her first experiences, especially of not being able to go about her own interests without her little brother tagging along:

> I was the eldest of five children. But I have very few memories of my early childhood in which my brother does not play a part. I remember my second birthday party and I remember spoiling my new red shoes by going out in the snow that winter. Then in the spring [1904] Richard was born, and very soon Margaret and Richard were expected to do everything together.[6]

Her parents actively encouraged Margaret's older-sister role, even allowing her to name her sister, Katherine, who was

Margaret with younger brother Richard. Margaret was often charged with the responsibility of watching over Richard.

in her autobiography. He got interested in an experiment on "briquettes," the forerunners of charcoal briquettes now used in barbecue pits and camp stoves. He took trips to a plant that made bricks. He bought two cows and watched the chart of their milk production. He invested in limburger cheese that nobody else in his family liked to eat. He watched the progress of a pretzel factory. "Year after year he played . . . games with industrial enterprises that could not be made to succeed but that could be made to fail less disastrously."[5] Although Margaret respected her father and felt very grown up in her understanding of his worries, she missed his attention and company. He called her his favorite, but his preoccupations kept him from knowing her very well or meeting her need for affection.

Margaret's Little Brother

In her autobiography, Margaret remembers what it was like to be expected to do everything with her brother.

"We used to have our supper together, wearing white nightclothes (with feet) and eating cereal or, on Sunday night, browis [mush] made of the dried remains of Saturday's Boston brown bread and baked beans soaked in hot milk. We were taught to sing the same songs together until it became obvious that while Richard's voice was true and clear, I had no voice at all. We even were dressed alike in blue coats with brass buttons and round stiff berets, and I passionately wanted a hat, but it was only when I was seven that I got permission to wear an old embroidered hat that a young aunt had left behind.

Richard was my little brother. He was valiant in my defense, standing in front of me and proclaiming, 'You let my sister be!' But he was also frail, and his frequent illnesses reinforced my father's overprotectiveness toward his only son. I have a few memories of genuine battles—there was a doll he smashed and the broken latch to my door at the farm, which he battered with a hammer, and once I was spanked because I had hit him. But in general our life together was placid and unexciting. Most of the pranks we played were my inventions, and whenever he tried to conceal any of our misdeeds he would blush scarlet under his fair skin, for he was embarrassingly truthful."

Margaret and Richard in Nantucket in 1911.

born in 1906. She always remembered Katherine's first and only Christmas because of the fur-dressed doll placed under the tree for the baby, who was then six months old.

A few months later, tragedy struck the family when Katherine suddenly died. The family never really recovered. Her father experienced a deep sense of loss that did not go away when Elizabeth was born in 1909, or when a third sister, Priscilla, was born in 1911. Her mother, too, was affected, and never took as much interest in her children after Katherine's death. Although Emily had written thirteen notebooks on Margaret's babyhood, and four on Richard's, she asked Margaret to keep the notebooks on Elizabeth and Priscilla. After Priscilla's birth, Emily went into a period of depression and for a while lived in Bucks County, away from the family.

Caring for "the Babies"

Like the rest of the family, Margaret called Elizabeth and Priscilla "the babies" even after they were well grown up. In some ways, she said, she thought of her sisters as "her children," whom she could observe and teach and cultivate and give "everything she has missed."[7] She wrote in *Blackberry Winter*:

> My care for my younger sisters fitted in with the role I chose for myself as a kind of stage manager at family festivals. It was a role that appealed to me. . . . What gave me the greatest pleasure, especially in later years, was arranging the settings within which Priscilla could display her beauty, Dick

could sing, and Elizabeth could play and dance for our enjoyment.

During all the years while we were growing up I was fascinated by the contrasts between my sisters. Elizabeth was enthusiastic, loving, and devoted. Priscilla was more self-centered and was devastatingly honest about her motives.[8]

Margaret's early maturity and her experiences in note-taking sharpened her eye for detail and comparison, which would carry over to her career in science. When telling how she became an anthropologist, she later wrote that her ability to compare made her interested in those who did not fit into their society or culture:

> From my earliest childhood I compared my own family with the kinds of

Edward Mead with Elizabeth in 1911.

families I heard about, learned about in songs, and read about in books. I thought seriously about the ways our family resembled other families, real and fictional, and sometimes sadly about the ways we did not fit into the expected pattern.[9]

Early Education

When Margaret was ten, the Meads bought a farm near Buckingham in Bucks County, Pennsylvania. This move influenced Margaret's early religious education. Margaret's parents and grandmother did not attend church, but Margaret was fascinated by religion. On her own, Margaret began to attend services at the Episcopal church in Buckingham. Although her parents did not share her enthusiasm for religious practices, Margaret felt at home with the Episcopal rector, Mr. Bell, and his daughter, Miss Lucia, and chose to be baptized in 1912. Her faith continued to give her inner strength throughout her entire life.

Most of Margaret's education took place at home, although she occasionally attended formal schools as well. Her father, who had won a Kappa key for public-speaking skills, insisted that she practice looking him in the eye while she gave her

A Family on the Move

The Meads lived first in Hammonton, New Jersey, and then in towns in Pennsylvania—and on a farm in Bucks County. Margaret opens her autobiography, Blackberry Winter, *with a general comment on her family's moves from city to city.*

"For me, moving and staying at home, traveling and arriving, are all of a piece. The world is full of homes in which I have lived for a day, a month, a year, or much longer. . . . From the time I can first remember, I knew that we had not always lived where we were living then—in Hammonton, New Jersey, where we had moved so that Mother could work on her doctoral thesis. I knew that I had spent my first summer at a resort. . . . I knew also that we had lived on St. Mark's Square, Philadelphia, because the next winter we lived near St. Mark's Square and still knew people who lived there.

Every winter we went to live in or near Philadelphia so that Father would not have to travel too far or stay in the city on the nights that he lectured at the University. From the time I was seven years old, we went somewhere for the summer, too. So we moved four times a year, because for the fall and spring we returned to the house in Hammonton."

speeches. Her mother encouraged Margaret in her presentation of a Shakespeare festival that featured madrigal singing and the casket scene from *The Merchant of Venice*. Her grandmother's inspiration led her to write long letters, which became another lifetime habit. In one section of *Blackberry Winter* she analyzes the nature of her instruction:

> Some years we went to school. Other years we stayed at home and Grandma taught us. . . . I spent two years in kindergarten, one year—but only half days—in the fourth grade, and six years in high school. If I had not very much wanted to go to school or if I had been a sickly child, probably I would have spent even less time in school. . . . My family deeply disapproved of any school that kept children chained to their desks, indoors, for long hours every day.
> Kindergarten—the one I attended

was a private kindergarten in the home of well-to-do people with a large house—was an expression of the most modern ideas about education. The training of eye and hand, learning about color and form and pattern by sewing with bright wools, cutting and pasting, and stringing brightly colored beads made of different materials, and singing in time to rhythmic play— these were all activities that my grandmother and mother and father regarded as good for children.[10]

Education meant more than books to the Mead family. Cooperation in all the family projects was also of prime importance. Margaret learned to cook and contribute to the village newspaper. She worked hard in the fields on their farm. Her diverse experiences included working with the threshers, learning how to top shocks of wheat as it was done in Ohio, and then "showing the men how to do it

Mead (middle row, far left) at Buckingham Friends School, where she graduated as valedictorian among her small class of four students.

Margaret had a quick mind and emanated a sense of enthusiasm and forcefulness. People who met her seemed to know that she was special.

full term. From 1916 to 1918 she attended a prep school in Doylestown. She graduated from high school for the second time at Holmquist School in New Hope, Pennsylvania, where she transferred for the year 1919-1920 so she could take German, a college-entrance requirement.

By this time she had reached her adult size of a little over five feet, two inches tall and less than 100 pounds. She had a head of curly, golden brown hair, deep-set brown eyes under straight brows, a boyish walk, and very small hands. She always wore her glasses, and she was always ready to debate on any subject. Her enthusiasm and forcefulness expressed both aggressiveness and vulnerability. She was optimistic and motherly, and had an incredibly quick mind and great determination. Everyone she met knew she was special, and she often took advantage of the fact that people liked to do things for her—her laundry, her typing, her chores and the various jobs she collected by her involvement in projects.

without making them mad."[11]

In the years 1913 to 1915, when she was twelve to fourteen years old, Margaret's formal schooling began in earnest with high school at the Buckingham Friends School in Bucks County. During this time World War I had started in Europe and Margaret, characteristically, daydreamed about the German armies marching through their wheat fields, fantasizing in her valedictory address on what might have happened "If Germany Had. . . ." Margaret's graduating class at Buckingham Friends School consisted of four students. The three others graduated as salutatorian, class poet, and class historian.

The next year she went on to the Bucks County Public High School for the

A Change in Plans?

There was no question in Margaret's mind that she would go to college just as her mother and her grandmother had done. Attendance at her mother's alma mater, Wellesley College in Massachusetts, had seemed like a foregone conclusion. After an exciting year at Holmquist School, she felt capable and academically well prepared. Then, in the spring of 1920, one of her father's private ventures failed, and he announced that he did not have enough money to send Margaret to college.

2 College and Career—Meeting the Right People

In 1920, Margaret and her mother did not accept her father's excuse that he had too little money to send her to college. Her mother and she plotted together to interest her father in sending her to DePauw University in central Indiana, where he had graduated. The plan worked, and he said he could find the money. Margaret immediately set about choosing her college wardrobe and packing boxes of books for the intellectual feast of college.

Margaret's personal life was full as well. Margaret had dated and secretly became engaged to Luther Cressman, the younger brother of a teacher at the Buckingham Friends School. Luther had graduated from Pennsylvania State College, where he studied Latin and Greek and

Mead became engaged to Luther Cressman (left), the younger brother of a teacher at Buckingham Friends School, but kept the news from family and friends. She later described their secret engagement as the living out of a romantic daydream.

prepared for the ministry in the Lutheran church. After graduation, he joined the Reserve Officers Training Corps (ROTC). At the end of World War I, when Luther came home from the army and Margaret went on to her sixth year in high school in New Hope, they told their parents, but none of their friends, about their engagement. In her autobiography, Margaret categorized her secret engagement, along with reading forbidden books, as the living out of a romantic daydream.

DePauw

Margaret left Luther and Pennsylvania for DePauw University in the fall of 1920. She looked forward to devoting herself to her studies. She soon discovered, however, that the university did not match her dreams. DePauw University, she wrote bitingly,

> was a college to which students had come for fraternity life, for football games, and for establishing the kind of rapport with other people that would make them good rotarians in later life and their wives good members of the garden club.[12]

Margaret despised the student body's emphasis on Greek-letter societies (fraternities and sororities) that she felt promoted a sense of privilege and conformity. She was shocked to see students subordinate their studies to thoughts of clothes, etiquette, and parties. She was more shocked to discover that Jews and Catholics were automatically excluded from the letter societies. She herself was not invited to join any of the clubs or

In 1920 Mead left for DePauw University with high hopes and aspirations, but was soon disappointed.

sororities and spent an isolated year. When she looked back on her experience, she wrote:

> During the year I studied at DePauw, I did not deny that I was hurt, nor did I pretend to myself that I would have refused the chance to be accepted by a sorority. The truth is, I would not have known enough to refuse. And once inside, it is quite possible that I would have been as unseeing as the rest. As it was, what particularly offended me as the year wore on was the contrast between the vaunted democracy of the Middle West and the blatant, strident artificiality of the Greek letter societies on that midwestern campus, the harshness of the rules that prevented my father's classmates from even addressing a hospitable word to me.[13]

Misfits in Society

Many years after Mead had spent her year feeling like a misfit at DePauw University, she wrote in her book Family *about the process by which society encourages conformity.*

"Wherever a boy grows up, he must learn to leave home without fear, leaving behind him the old battles of childhood, and learn to return home from school or work or an assignment in a far city or overseas ready to treat his parents differently. . . . If he succeeds, he may open that path to others. If he fails, others coming after him may have a harder time.

For the young boy who rebels against the choices that have been made for him—refuses the wife who has been chosen in his name, deserts the craft to which he has been apprenticed, leaves the school or college to which he has been sent—the battle is a lonely one. . . . The problems girls face, the world over, are not those that confront their brothers, but very different ones. For the adolescent girl may still feel like a child or she may still long to roam the hills with her brothers as she did when she was a child, but now, unlike a child, she can conceive. And long before she has the discretion or the judgment to choose among suitors or to weigh the temptation of the moment against her hopes for the future, her body, outstripping her imagination, or her imagination, outstripping her physical readiness, may involve her in an irrevocable act. The boy who breaks his bow string, turns tail in battle, hesitates before an order, or fails in school can still retrieve his losses by stringing the bow better, returning to school, learning to obey and to command. But for the girl herself and for society, the change is irreversible. It does not matter whether the child she has conceived is lost immediately after conception, whether it is born in wedlock or out of wedlock, whether it lives or dies. The event cannot be set aside. One more child, if it lives, will have started life in one way and not in another, and the girl herself can go on, but she cannot begin afresh."

Transfer to Barnard College

At the end of her freshman year, Mead transferred from DePauw to New York City, to the women's college of Columbia University, Barnard, for the rest of her undergraduate work. There, college life matched her ideals. She lived with several other women students in an apartment and made friends with other women who wrote poetry, agitated for social justice, and centered their lives on intellectual interests. They decorated their doors with poetry and sympathized with the downtrodden. After their drama teacher referred to them in disgust as the "Ash Can Cats," they adopted that name in defiance.

Of Mead's years at Barnard, her biographer, Jane Howard, writes:

> Margaret did not sneak in through the windows after curfew. Margaret did not flirt with the young men across the courtyard who threw pennies into the windows of 606 when the Ash Can Cats

played "I Left My Love in Avalon" or "Apple Blossom Time" on the phonograph. Margaret did put a framed picture of her brother Dick on the desk of a classmate who had no boyfriend, to give her some idea of how it might feel to have an admirer. Margaret did not have to wonder how it felt; Margaret had Luther. . . . Luther was Margaret's stalwart and unrivaled fiancé.[14]

Mead respected her Barnard professors. After her English professor, William Brewster, told her she would never be a writer, she decided to major in psychology.

She chose to do her senior project on how immigration affected the results of intelligence (IQ) tests. But when she decided to take a class in anthropology from a Germany-born professor, Franz Boas, she made a decision that turned her in the direction of her life work.

In her anthropology class she learned how field workers collected artifacts and recorded stories of long-lived traditions in primitive areas. When they returned, the

Mead pictured with two members of the Ash Can Cats, Leonie Adams (left) and Eleanor Pelham Kortheuer (right).

anthropologists wrote books, or ethnographies, on the exotic ceremonies and events they had observed. When people read these ethnographies, they found out how people in other cultures married, raised their children, and made their living.

Professor Boas had begun his work in anthropology just after it had begun to be considered a "social" science; that is, a science that studies human behavior. Some American anthropologists had been advocating eugenics, the idea that certain races inherited certain traits that made them somehow superior. Professor Boas was opposed to the theory. While living among American Indians, he had become convinced that heredity was only one influence on the formation of any person.

Mead liked Boas's egalitarian [equal-minded] attitude as well as the field of anthropology. She became friends with Boas's laboratory assistant, Ruth Benedict, who encouraged Mead to pursue field work among primitive peoples. Mead decided to work for a Ph.D. in anthropology. With Professor Boas's advice, she chose to write her thesis on a comparison of Polynesian cultures.

In the summer of 1924, the British Association for the Advancement of Science accepted Mead's proposal to speak at their Toronto meeting on her study of the tattooing practices of Polynesians. After the meetings Mead joined the small groups who were discussing their research on remote islands and in faraway jungles. This spurred her to do her own field work.

Professor Franz Boas introduced Mead to anthropology. His work inspired her to enter the field of anthropology and obtain a Ph.D. at Barnard.

Graduate Work and Marriage

All during their college years, Margaret and Luther continued their engagement. They married on September 23, 1923, following her graduation from Barnard. The ceremony was held at the same Episcopal church in which Margaret had been baptized. The bridal party dressed in simple white dresses and large scoop hats with tulle bows. Margaret did not become Mrs. Luther Cressman; instead, she kept her maiden name. Already believing she would be famous she wanted to be known as Margaret Mead.

The newlyweds drove a borrowed car to their honeymoon on Cape Cod and, having been engaged for five years, felt right at home together. Then they rented

Beginning the Study of Anthropology

In her biography of her friend, Ruth Benedict, *Mead recalls how, with Ruth's help, she got off to a good start in her study of anthropology.*

"I was the child of social scientists and the basic ideas of the independence of race, language, and culture, as well as the importance of the comparative method, were already familiar to me. What was new to me was the emphasis on the intricate details of primitive cultures, a kind of detail of which there was no hint in the work of the comparative socioeconomists . . . who had been my parents' teachers. Following Ruth Benedict's suggestion I spent long evenings when I was baby-sitting memorizing Australian and Toda kinship systems or copying out Northwest Coast designs until I had the feel of those marvelously dissected sharks and eagles in my fingertips.

She brought home to us also the desperate urgency of doing anthropological field work before the last precious and irretrievable memories of traditional American Indian cultures were carried to the grave. She herself had done her first field work in the summer of 1922 among the Mononga Valley Serano, one of the Shoshonean groups of southern California. This was the situation she found:

'No old shaman or priest survives. The annual fiesta is still kept up in a modified form, and . . . the Reservation . . . depended on a shaman of the desert Cahuilla for some of the old dances and shamanistic performances. . . . It is largely by guesswork that they can give the meaning of any of the ceremonial songs; and any religious connotation in such practices as rock-painting, for instance, is now unknown.'"

Anthropologist Ruth Benedict. Benedict encouraged Mead to pursue field work among native peoples in the hopes of preserving and recording the unique customs of the traditional cultures.

Following her graduation from Barnard and their five-year engagement, Mead and Luther Cressman married. Already confident that she would become famous, Mead (left, with Grandmother at wedding) kept her maiden name. During Mead's studies at Barnard, Luther attended the General Theological Seminary (right).

an apartment near Columbia University and settled into being students.

Mead wrote her dissertation on *The Question of Cultural Stability in Polynesia*, which was an examination of the interrelationship of canoe-building, house-building, and tattooing in Polynesia. The more she read, the more she wanted to go to Polynesia to do field work among the people she studied.

To make this possible, in 1925 she applied for a fellowship from the National Research Council, and Professor Boas backed her application. Unfortunately, the fellowship would only support her while she was actually in the field; she would still need to travel eight thousand miles to get there. When her father heard that she might have to do her work among the American Indians instead, which she did not want to do, he gave her the money she needed to travel to the Pacific.

Despite meeting some opposition to her plan to work in a wild and primitive country, Mead made only two compromis-es. She agreed to go to American Samoa instead of to Polynesia, so that if she got sick, she would be able to contact the American navy, whose ships made coaling stops in Pago Pago (pronounced pahngo, pahngo) Samoa. She also agreed with Professor Boas to study adolescent behavior rather than overall changes in the entire culture.

Pioneer Field Trip to the Pacific

Both Luther and Margaret completed their theses before the news came on May 1, 1925, that she had been awarded the fellowship. They spent the summer in separate preparations. While Luther got ready to go to England for further study, Mead prepared for Samoa. She took her inoculations, and purchased a camera, pencils and notebooks, cotton dresses, and spare glasses for her trip. She bought tobacco, beads, and trinkets because as an anthropologist she would be expected to pay her informants [people from whom anthropologists get their information]. She also interviewed for and received a job as assistant curator at the American Museum of Natural History, a position that would begin after she returned from the field.

Even the disappointing news that the National Research Council had decided not to advance her the money for her preparatory expenses did not lessen her enthusiasm. Undaunted, she took the train to San Francisco, stopping in Arizona for a few days of sightseeing in the Grand Canyon with Ruth Benedict, and sailed for the South Pacific.

Mead knew very little about what she was getting into or how to proceed. She later wrote in her autobiography:

> I had read Ruth's description of [the Zuni Indians] . . . the fierceness of the bedbugs and the difficulties of managing food, but I knew little about how she went about her work. Professor Boas always spoke of the Kwakiutl as 'my dear friends,' but this was not followed by anything that helped me to know what it was like to live among them. . . .
>
> I had a half hour's instruction in which Professor Boas told me that I must be willing to seem to waste time just sitting about and listening. . . . During the summer he also wrote me a letter in which he once more cautioned me to be careful of my health.[15]

Mead was certain, however, that she was trained in what to look for, if not in how to record what she saw. She knew she was going with the right attitude, ready to see people as complete human beings with their own ways of life. She might not know what she would do if she felt lonely or frustrated, but she was on her own.

A Beginning in the South Pacific

Mead's trip to Samoa included a transfer and two-week layover in Honolulu. There she was met by May Dillingham Freer, a Wellesley College classmate of her mother. The Dillinghams were influential enough to find both a driver to take Mead to study at the museum each day and a tutor, Craighill Handy, to give her lessons in the

Mead on the eve of departure for her trip to Samoa in 1925. Mead departed on her journey with a sense of excitement and anticipation.

Lolo, chief in Vaitogi. During her stay in Vaitogi, Mead lived in the chief's household.

Samoan language while she waited for the ship that would take her to her tiny tropical island.

Two weeks later, she sailed with a few additions to her field supplies—a hundred squares of muslin to use as handkerchiefs if the children had runny noses, a silk pillow, and a lamp.

When she arrived in Pago Pago, the main port of American Samoa, her letter of introduction from the U.S. surgeon general put her in touch with the chief navy nurse, Miss Hodgeson, and a language tutor, Pepe, who spoke both English and Samoan. She lived in the hotel

for six weeks, unable to pay her bill because her check from the National Research Council was late. But she put her time to good use, memorizing vocabulary by the hour.

She had hoped she could start her field work in Pago Pago, but she saw that this port was far too westernized to study as a primitive culture. Instead she made arrangements to catch a steamer to a small village on another island. "Finally," she writes in *Blackberry Winter*,

> the boat arrived again. And now . . . I was able to move to a village, Vaitogi, and to live in the household of a chief who enjoyed entertaining visitors. It was there I had all my essential training in how to manage Samoan etiquette. His daughter Fa'amotu was my constant companion. We slept together on a pile of mats at the end of the sleeping house. We were given privacy from the rest of the family by a tapa [bark cloth] curtain.[16]

But living with a chief's family in Vaitogi was not satisfactory for Mead's study, either. From Vaitogi she went on to Tau, which was more old fashioned and had a medical post where she could live. She took notes on all her experiences, falling back on her childhood exercise of taking notes on her sisters. And, as had been her custom from the time she could write, she brought those distant scenes to life for her family, friends, and professors by writing long letters about her expeditions, the village dances, and the Samoan ceremonies.

3 Six Months in Samoa

Mead's ten days in Vaitogi ended on November 7, 1925, with her steamer trip to Tau, Manu'a, where she found nearly seventy adolescent girls who would be her informants on adolescent life. A week later, on November 14, she described her field work site in a letter home to Professor Boas and her family:

> As far as I know now I will be here the rest of my stay in Samoa. The whole location is ideal for my problem. Tau is an island 8 miles by 11 miles and 32 miles in circumference and 12 miles from the other two islands in the group, Ofu and Olesega, which rise sheer from the sea and look as if they were about a mile away. There are four villages on Tau: Fitiuta, 8 miles away at the other end of the island, and three villages right here, Luma (where I live) and Siufaga and Faleasao. The first two touch boundaries at the common church and Faleasao is about half a mile away over quite a steep trail. The dispensary is the only *papalagi* (foreign) house here. Even the church is built in Samoan fashion with the addition of whitewashed wooden walls. There is a store which charges exorbitant prices for bad food and that is all. There are between 900 and 1000 peo-

ple in these villages which are right at my very doorstep.[17]

Soon she was acquainted with the small tropical island with its round, thatch-roofed houses, its mission church and tiny hospital, and its thousand brown-skinned people in four villages. She stayed in the medical post, a frame building in which Edward Holt lived with his wife and two children, and which also contained his small dispensary [pharmacy]. Her room on half the back porch could be either divided by a curtain or opened up as an office.

Mead's Schedule of Field Work

Mead now began to fill in charts with the names of sixty-eight girls whom she would use in her study. She noted their family structures—whether their parents were alive, living together, or divorced; the number of brothers, sisters, half-brothers, and half-sisters they had; and which relatives they lived with.

To help her evaluate what her informants told her, Mead invented IQ, or "intelligence," tests that did not require read-

Life in Tau, Samoa

In Coming of Age in Samoa, *Mead describes the sights and sounds of the island of Tau in Samoa.*

"The insistent roar of the reef seems muted to an undertone for the sounds of a waking village. Babies cry, a few short wails before sleepy mothers give them the breast. Restless little children roll out of their sheets and wander down to the beach to freshen their faces in the sea. Boys, bent upon early fishing, start collecting the tackle and go to rouse their more laggard companions. Fires are lit, here and there, the white smoke visible against the paleness of the dawn. The whole village, sheeted and frowsy, stirs, rubs its eyes, and stumbles toward the beach. . . . Girls stop to giggle over some young ne'er-do-well who escaped during the night from an angry father's pursuit and to venture a shrewd guess that the daughter knew more about his presence than she told. The boy who is taunted by another, who has succeeded him in his sweetheart's favor, grapples with his rival, his foot slipping in the wet sand. From the other end of the village comes a long drawn-out, piercing wail. A messenger has just brought word of the death of some relative in another village. Half-clad, unhurried women, with babies at their breasts, or astride their hips, pause in their tale of Losa's outraged departure from her father's house to the greater kindness in the home of her uncle, to wonder who is dead. Poor relatives whisper their requests to rich relatives, men make plans to set a fish trap together, a woman begs a bit of yellow dye from a kinswoman, and through the village sounds the rhythmic tattoo which calls the young men together."

The round, thatch-roofed houses typical of Samoa.

ing. Giving directions in Samoan, she asked the girls to name colors, remember strings of numbers, substitute geometrical figures for digits, name opposites, and interpret pictures.

Her weeks followed a simple schedule. On weekdays, Faleasao, her helper, who spoke only Samoan, came promptly at eight and stayed until eleven, helping Mead talk to the girls. After Faleasao left, Mead had lunch with the Holts, slept through the hottest part of the day, began the interviews again at 3:30, ate supper with the Holts at 5:00, and then either typed and organized her notes or developed photographic film until midnight.

Faleasao came at six on Sunday mornings to wake Margaret up for the long, hot walk to church in the parish of the London Missionary Society. After Sunday services, the girls she was studying went bathing in the sea, and Margaret wrote on the porch until they returned carrying pails of water hung from poles on their shoulders.

Mead recorded everything she could learn about the culture. She found that the Samoan girls were responsible for selecting and preparing food, weeding the garden, selecting the best bananas or breadfruit for food, and cutting coconuts. They made puddings using red-hot stones for cooking. They fished at night by torchlight, lured octopus with a stick, and gathered large crabs. Their special skill was weaving mats of bark or leaves for use as rugs, sleeping mats, workplace pads, or roof thatch. Everyone wore mats and gave them as gifts.

The girls developed the skill of making dancing skirts from grass fibers. They also made clothing and household goods, for which they had to gather, then scrape and pound, paper mulberry bark to make the cloth called *tapa*.

A Samoan woman scrapes mulberry bark to make tapa, *a cloth used to make clothing and household goods.*

General Cultural Patterns

Mead also observed and recorded general cultural values, such as the Samoan emphasis on courtesy language, and taboos. The courtesy language contained special vocabularies for each rank of chief and age group. Everyone needed to know their own words, the chief's words, and the courtesy phrases of welcome; what to say when passing in front of someone; and what was expected in the event of birth, miscarriage, sexual intercourse, death, or surgery. Taboos forbade brothers and sisters to touch each other after reaching the age of ten. They could not talk to each other in familiar terms, mention any private matters, or even be together in their own homes unless they were with a large group.

Samoan people spent most of their time either fishing or gathering tropical foods from the interior of their island. When a young married couple needed a new home, special carpenters would build it. Then a sacred oven full of food was prepared, and fine mats were presented to the carpenters as gifts. Since families sat cross-legged on mats that covered dirt floors strewn with small coral stones, these gifts of mats were much prized.

Even in this old-fashioned village, native customs were already mixed with Western ones. Women still made *tapa*, but they wrapped themselves in cotton sheets to protect their heads and skin from the torrid sun. Women still wore *lavalava* [a simple, straight body wrap], but the missionaries had also introduced skirts and shirts. Boys still painted their faces and wore grass dancing skirts (*sivas*), but they also were learning how to write. The mis-

Mead and Fa'amoto in Samoan attire. In Samoa, many native customs, including clothing styles, had become mixed with Western ones.

sionaries had also taught the girls how to use a sewing machine, embroider, wash, and iron in the European way. To the Samoan games of climbing palm trees and swimming, the missionaries added cricket.

The missionaries had introduced Christian observances, such as Christmas, and everyone made and wrapped presents for relatives and friends. New Year's was an even more popular holiday, celebrated with lavish eating and a late-night jamboree on the seashore. The teenage girls Mead studied talked endlessly about the noise and fun.

Life of a Samoan Girl

In Coming of Age in Samoa, *Mead describes the life of the young Samoan girl.*

"In the house the girl's principal task is to learn to weave. She has to master several different techniques. First, she learns to weave palm branches where the central rib of the leaf serves as a rim to her basket or an edge to her mat and where the leaflets are already arranged for weaving. From palm leaves she first learns to weave a carrying basket, made of half a leaf, by plaiting the leaflets together and curving the rib into a rim. Then she learns to weave the Venetian blinds which hang between the house posts, by laying one-half leaf upon another and plaiting the leaflets together. More difficult are the floor mats, woven of four great palm leaves, and the floor platters with their intricate designs. There are also fans to make, simple two-strand weaves which she learns to make quite well, more elaborate twined ones which are the prerogatives of older and more skilled weavers. Usually some older woman in the household trains a girl to weave and sees to it that she makes at least one of each kind of article, but she is only called upon to produce in quantity the simpler things, like the Venetian blinds. From the pandanus she learns to weave the common floor mats, one or two types of the more elaborate bed mats, and then, when she is thirteen or fourteen, she begins her first fine mat. The fine mat represents the high point of Samoan weaving virtuosity. Woven of the finest quality of pandanus which has been soaked and baked and scraped to a golden whiteness and paperlike thinness, of strands a sixteenth of an inch in width, these mats take a year or two years to weave and are as soft and pliable as linen. They form the unit of value, and must always be included in the dowry of the Bride. Girls seldom finish a fine mat until they are nineteen or twenty, but once the mat has been started, wrapped up in a coarser one, it rests among the rafters, a testimony to the girl's industry and manual skill."

The End of Her First Field Trip

In June of 1926 it was time for Mead to return to Pago Pago, where she had first arrived nearly eight months before. As she packed her notes and pictures, she was sure her knowledge of Samoan culture would be a worthwhile contribution to anthropology. She was ready to write about "her" people. She already had a theory that her observations about the teenage girls could be presented as a cross section of the whole culture, one that explained how the Samoan people interacted. She

Mead with a young Samoan boy, Paulo. Mead chronicled her Samoan experiences and observations in Coming of Age in Samoa.

was actually inventing a new kind of anthropology—one that would be used very extensively by the mid-1900s.

She had, moreover, some theories about education. In the book she based on her Samoan work, *Coming of Age in Samoa,* she compared the easygoing attitude of the Samoan girls with the rebellion of American adolescents. She concluded that American adolescents rebelled because their parents tried to make them lead such restricted lives:

> We must turn all our educational efforts to training our children for the choices which will confront them. Education, in the home even more than at school, instead of being a special pleading for one regime, a desperate attempt to form one particular habit of mind which will withstand all outside influences, must be a preparation for those very influences. . . . The child who is to choose wisely must be healthy in mind and body. . . . And even more importantly, this child of the future must have an open mind. The home must cease to plead an ethical cause or a religious belief with smiles or frowns, caresses or threats. The children must be taught how to think, not what to think, . . . they must be taught tolerance, just as today they are taught intolerance. They must be taught that many ways are open to them, . . . and that upon them and upon them alone lies the burden of choice.[18]

Margaret's experience in Samoa made her an advocate of teaching tolerance. She asked, "Will we, who have the knowledge of many ways, leave our children free to choose among them?"[19]

The Voyage Home

In a brief visit with her adopted family, that of the chief of Vaitogi, she realized how homesick she was, thousands of miles from New York. She was eager, too, to meet Luther, and later Ruth Benedict, for a tour of Europe.

The ocean voyage from Samoa to the United States was scheduled to take six weeks. On the way to Sydney, Australia, the ship ran into a severe storm that foundered eleven other ships. Mead's captain and crew, however, brought her safely to Sydney. Luther's cousins met her with flowers and took her to a concert, and then she boarded the luxury liner, the *Chitral*, that would take her to Marseille, France.

A dock strike in England kept the *Chitral* from sailing to a scheduled stop in Tasmania to pick up a load of apples. Instead it remained docked in Sydney for several days. Mead had too little money to shop or to stay in a Sydney hotel, so she stayed aboard and met some of the other passengers. One of these was a psychologist from New Zealand, Reo Fortune, who was on his way to Cambridge University in England.

Mead later described the charged atmosphere in which they met:

> Both Reo and I were in a state of profound excitement. He was going to England to meet people who would understand what he was talking about, and I, just emerging from the field, was hungering and thirsting for communication. In many ways innocent and inexperienced, Reo was unlike anyone I had ever known. He had nev-

Mead, back home from the field, met Luther in France.

er seen a play professionally performed, he had never seen an original painting by a great artist or heard music played by a symphony orchestra. But to make up for the isolation in which New Zealanders lived in the days before modern communications, he had read deeply and with delight, ranging through the whole of English literature, and he had eagerly taken hold of whatever he could find on psychoanalysis. It was like meeting a stranger from another planet, but a stranger with whom I had a great deal in common.[20]

On the ship, which stopped in every port, Reo and Margaret talked at meals about their fields of study. They went to a masquerade party together and passed a day in Ceylon, and another in Sicily, enjoying each other's company. Finally, howev-

After returning home to New York, Mead began work as assistant curator of Ethnology at the American Museum of Natural History.

er, they parted in Marseille, France, where Margaret met Luther.

From Marseille Margaret and Luther traveled north through France. Luther had seen Paris and had no interest in seeing it again, and decided not to go. But Ruth was there, and Margaret, feeling that she and Ruth now had more than ever in common, enjoyed sharing her Samoan memories with her fellow anthropologist while they toured the city. They compared Ruth's idea of psychological patterns with Reo's psychological insights, and as Margaret said of Ruth in her biography, "began a discussion that continued for many years."[21]

Luther joined her and Ruth for the trip to Italy to hear anthropological presentations at a meeting of the Congress of the Americanists in Rome. Reo crossed over from Cambridge to see them off when they boarded their boat in Paris, ready to sail at last for New York.

A New Direction for Margaret's Life

In New York the couple's life took a new and unexpected direction. While he was in England, Luther had decided to switch from the ministry to anthropology and he got a job teaching at the City College of New York. Margaret began her daily work as Assistant Curator of Ethnology in a tiny office at the American Museum of Natural History, part of her work being the writing of her book, *Coming of Age in Samoa*. It was at this time that she learned she was unable to have children. With Luther busy teaching, and her mind on Samoa, Margaret began to rethink her dream of being Luther's wife.

She also had a hard time forgetting Reo and wrote to him at Cambridge. In their letters Margaret and Reo planned a

Babysitting in Samoa

In Samoa, Mead says in a letter published in Letters from the Field, *most of the babysitting is done by young children.*

"The chief nurse-maid is usually a child of six or seven who is not strong enough to lift a baby over six months old, but who can carry the child straddling the left hip, or on the small of the back. . . . Their diminutive [small, young] nurses do not encourage children to walk, as babies who can walk about are more complicated charges. . . .

I have known them to intersperse their remarks every two or three minutes with, 'Keep still,' 'Sit still,' 'Keep your mouths shut,' 'Stop that noise,' uttered quite mechanically although all of the little ones present may have been behaving as quietly as a row of intimidated mice. On the whole, this last requirement of silence is continually mentioned and never enforced. The little nurses are more interested in peace than in forming the characters of their small charges and when a child begins to howl, it is simply dragged out of earshot of its elders. No mother will ever exert herself to discipline a younger child if an older one can be made responsible."

meeting in Germany. In the spring of 1927, travel was so inexpensive Margaret could spend eleven weeks abroad for only $325. She arranged to go on a tour of German museums to study their collections of Oceanic art. Reo came late to their planned rendezvous, but he did come. After three days together in Berlin, they agreed to marry.

Back in New York, Luther received Margaret's letter with the news that "they had no future together."[22] When Margaret came back to New York, Luther considerately moved out. They were divorced through proceedings in Mexico.

In her autobiography, Margaret wrote about the end of their marriage:

I returned to New York to say good-bye to Luther. We spent a placid week together, unmarred by reproaches or feelings of guilt. At the end of it, he sailed for England to see the girl whom he later married, and who became the mother of his daughter.[23]

Although it was the end of Margaret's marriage, it was just the beginning of her career.

4 Working with Five More Cultures

When *Coming of Age in Samoa* was published in 1928, it brought Mead fame. Within the next six years she added to her celebrity status by observing and describing five more cultures and writing a second best-seller. During this period, she drew widespread attention with her innovative and collaborative approaches to writing ethnologies, when the prevailing practice of the time was for each anthropologist to jealously guard his or her territory and refuse to share information.

While Mead waited for her book to appear on bookstore shelves, she resumed her work as a museum curator, renewed her acquaintance with her college friends, the Ash Can Cats, and promoted her coming book.

Margaret's decision to marry Reo was complicated by his New Zealand citizenship. They planned to work together in an Australian colony in New Guinea, so he could apply for his funds as a graduate of Australian schools. Margaret also wanted to find funding so she would be free to work with Reo. She succeeded in obtaining both a grant for field work in New Guinea from the Social Science Research Council and a year's leave of absence from the museum, from January 1929 to January 1930.

Margaret and Reo's long psychological discussions on the *Chitral* had given them many ideas on how to work together, but the goals of their grants were separate and distinct. Even so, Margaret hoped they could work together to apply psychology to their understanding of cultures, to provide better anthropological descriptions than those written using traditional techniques, which did not try to explain how people's minds worked. Margaret's proposed project was a follow-up to her Samoan work—a study of the mental development of young children and adolescent girls. She was now hoping to become even better known in the field of anthropology.

Plans materialized so fast that before Margaret actually saw her first book in print, she had to board the transcontinental train to San Francisco, in December of 1928, just before her twenty-seventh birthday, and sail for Australia to meet Reo. She was excited about her new marriage, and, as she later said, in *Letters from the Field*, exultant over having someone with whom she could share field work:

> I traveled alone across the Pacific. Reo met my ship in Auckland [New Zealand], where we married. From this time on, my intellectual life became a cooperative enterprise and the

excitement of intellectual discussion was part of my life in the field itself, not something to be shared in letters or much later, after the event.[24]

Learning About the Manus

They went almost immediately to Manus, which was in the Admiralty Islands, north of New Guinea, just below the equator and east of Samoa. At that time the area was legally protected by Australia but still had its own leaders and customs. Mead's unromantic observation about Australian rule in New Guinea was that

a hundred or so white men govern and exploit this vast country—find gold, plant great plantations, trade for shell, hide their failures in other lands, drink inordinately, run into debt, steal each other's wives, go broke and commit suicide or get rich—if they know how.[25]

Reo and Margaret found tutors to help them with the two languages they would need, Pidgin English and Manus. They settled in Peré Village, which consisted of about forty-three large, windowless houses, all built on stilts in a lagoon behind a large coral reef. They had their own, smaller house and a group of young boys and girls, led by a thirteen-year-old boy, Kilipak, to do the cooking and household chores. It was, Mead reported in a letter of January 10, 1929, "altogether a jolly household, infantile, happy, with Kilipak, a genius at organization, at the head."[26] They ate wild duck, pigeon, and possum; fish; and coconuts, papaya, pineapple, or taro [a starchy vegetable], all of which spoiled rapidly in the heat and had to be cooked or eaten immediate-

Manus children play in the lagoon outside the government rest house, where Mead first lived in Peré village.

Housekeeping in Manus

In January of 1929, Mead was on her second field trip, in Manus, New Guinea. She wrote a letter, published in Letters from the Field 1925-1975, *about their new home and helpers.*

"Kilipak 'Go to Pak' (an island), has been head cook. Kilipak is possibly thirteen, quick as a flash, son of the ruling family, a natural leader of men. Kilipak's promotion to cook promoted Sotoan, formerly mere kitchen knave who worked for his food alone, to the position of waiter and head *valet de chambre* [butler]. Sotoan is possibly twelve, mild, without authority, deprecatory in manner. And a new *monkey* (Pidgin English for "small boy"), who had not haunted the premises before, became assistant *valet de chambre*. They are so tiny that it takes two to fold a blanket. An even smaller *monkey*, Kapeli, also joined the forces. So the household headed by a boy of thirteen got under way. The procedure of the absent Manuwai was faithfully imitated by Kilipak; Sotoan strove to take on some of Kilipak's authority as butler and never forgot the vinegar, the quinine, the salt, and the hemoglobin bottles. And Kilipak next organized a band of ten-year-old girls to fetch the firewood. . . . Five tiny girls, wearing their little grass tails before and behind, set off in two small canoes, one outriggerless, fastened together to contain the firewood. On their return he shared a tiny bit of his tobacco with them and begged cigarette paper for the whole crew. . . . No one had more than a minimum of work to do, everyone was gay and happy, serious about their tasks, running away to run canoe races while I slept in the early afternoon. For water, wood and cooking I was well equipped."

Villagers board canoes during a ceremony.

A group of young girls at work. In Manus, where marriages were arranged for children, dress codes and rules about relations between the sexes were very rigid.

ly. With so much household help, Margaret could spend her time listening, observing, and taking notes.

Mead found the culture of Manus quite different from that of Samoa, though the food and occupations were the same on both islands. But where Samoans were warm and easygoing, the Manus were obsessively interested in making a profit by trading

> in markets with the people of distant islands for large objects like tree trunks and turtles and exchanges among themselves that focused on marriage payments in which indestructible valuables—dog's teeth, shell money, and in recent times, beads—were given in return for consumable food and clothing.[27]

Manus had no mission as Tau did. In her first letter from Peré, Mead described the appearance of a typical Manus man, "clad only in G-string, bracelets, armlets and woven belt, with a bag for his betel nut [a narcotic gum] and pepper leaf slung over his shoulder."[28] The women and girls wore grass "tails" front and back. Unlike the casual Samoans, the Manus were almost puritan in their adherence to dress codes and relations between the sexes.

The rigidity was in part due to the Manus religion. Marriages were arranged when the boy and girl were children. A wedding ritual centered around the payment of pigs and dogs' teeth for the bride. Everyone needed to be assured that the ghosts (spirits of dead relatives and friends) were satisfied with the payment and would not do anything bad to the bride, the groom, or their relatives. The wedding could be called off if the payment were not satisfactory, which might be decided by the fact, for example, that a pig had died or a child had become ill. When everyone was sure the ghosts were happy, the bride was dressed in her family's gifts for the groom's family—so many beads and feather combs she could scarcely be seen.

According to the Manus religion, trouble always had something to do with ghosts of the dead. If a little child died, the entire village would argue over which payments had not been made to one of the ghost's living relatives. To the villagers, Mead and Reo appeared to have some power over the spirits because when a child was delirious from malaria, they would give it quinine.

As Mead watched and listened, she began to think about the psychology of education in America and to make the comparisons she would include in her next book, *Growing Up in New Guinea*.

In Manus, she saw that every effort given to the children's earliest education was intended to make them physically strong and self-sufficient in their dangerous environment. "Clumsiness, physical uncertainty and lack of poise, is unknown among adults."[29] Any skill a child showed in swimming, diving, rowing, steering a canoe, climbing, or throwing was praised and noticed. Mead wrote, "There is not a child of five who can't swim well. A Manus child who couldn't swim would be as aberrant, as definitely subnormal as an American child of five who couldn't walk."[30]

Through the contrasts she saw between Manus children and other toddlers, Mead understood the Manus values and how these children became such strong, businesslike adults:

Mead with a group of Manus children. At an early age Manus children were taught the importance of physical strength and self-sufficiency in their often dangerous environment.

Mead with a young Manus child.

In Manus where property is sacred and one wails for lost property as for the dead, respect for property is taught children from their earliest years. Before they can walk they are rebuked and chastised for touching anything which does not belong to them. . . . All our possessions, fascinating red and yellow cans of food, photographic material, books, were safe from the two- and three-year-olds who would have been untamed vandals in a forest of loot in most societies.[31]

With adults placing such a strong value on successful property exchanges and payments, they had no need to make the children work. Children spent their days swimming, canoeing, throwing play spears, and swinging from the tall trees on thirty-foot vines far out over the water.

Mead tested the mental development of the Manus children by having them draw pictures, something the people of Peré village had never tried before. She gave them no models or instruction except to start with the older ones so that the little children could imitate them. They liked the drawing so well they would take new paper and pencils to bed with them and get up at dawn to draw. She discovered from their many pictures that they tried to draw only practical things they saw and used. They exhibited little or no "childish" imagination. This observation proved to her that their education made business-minded adults out of Manus children.

The Anthropologists Return to New York

Six months later, in July, Reo and Margaret left Manus. They had no reason to hurry back to New York, since Margaret's leave from the museum was to last through December, so they spent six weeks in Australia, where they heard about the work of an English anthropologist, Gregory Bateson, who was working among another primitive people of New Guinea.

Their arrival in New York shortly before the bank failures and stock-market losses of 1929 brought the first causes of tension between them—Margaret's fame and a lack of money. *Coming of Age in Samoa* was a best-seller, but the publisher realized scarcely any profit. Most of Reo's savings were lost in the crash, and the only money they had was from Margaret's account in the little Doylestown bank her father had recommended. Besides their other financial setbacks, the museum reduced her already-meager salary of $2,500 a year.

Margaret's success was a problem to

Reo. Because of his New Zealand cultural upbringing, he saw her fame as a reproach to his own lack of success. His upbringing also gave him different role expectations for Margaret than she had for herself as a career woman. He did not like her to spend long hours typing up her field notes, writing her book on the Manus, and keeping up her job at the museum.

On the other hand, he did not like to see her doing housework, either, and wished he could provide her with servants.

Their relationship suffered even more strain during the summer of 1930 on their field trip to Omaha, Nebraska. Margaret had agreed to do a study of Indian women after Ruth Benedict found funds for Reo to go with her. But Reo's informants were

Learning Sex Roles in Manus

Mead described the education of the Manus children in Growing Up in New Guinea, *her second best-seller. Here she speaks about the young girl's life:*

"Up to the time a little girl is five or six, she accompanies her father as freely as would her brother. She sleeps with her father, sometimes until she is seven or eight. By this time she is entering the region of tabu. If she is not engaged herself, younger sisters and cousins may be engaged, and she will be on terms of avoidance with the boys to whom they are betrothed. If she is engaged herself, there will likely be several men in the village from whom she must hide her face. She is no longer the careless child who rode upon her father's back into the very sanctuary of male life, the ship island. More and more her father tends to leave her at home for her younger brothers and sisters, or to go more staidily, babyless, about his business. But she is used to adult attention, dependent upon the sense of power which it gives her. Gradually deserted by her father, she comes to identify herself either with her mother or with some older woman of her kindred. . . . The older women are freer to teach the girls beadwork, to start them at work for their trousseaux. The younger women are more preoccupied with baby tending, which does not interest the little girls and in which their help is not enlisted. Little girls have no dolls and no patterns of playing with babies. We bought some little wooden statues from a neighboring tribe and it was the boys who treated them as dolls and crooned lullabies to them."

unsatisfactory, and Margaret felt depressed over the plight of the impoverished Indian women. Margaret wrote of "three strenuous, grueling months caught in a style of work . . . we were not used to, watching the sorrows of a fading culture."[32] They grew physically tired, too, for because of the dust and heat, they had to do their work at night.

Back in New York, Reo at last finished his doctoral dissertation, and Margaret got a check from the sale of *Coming of Age in Samoa.* With just enough money to make expenses for their trip, they began to press toward their goal of partnership in field work. Margaret now had a plan to study the psychological "conditioning of the social personalities of the two sexes." She hoped that she could throw light on sex differences through more work in New Guinea.

Third Field Trip to the South Pacific

Margaret and Reo set out again for new Guinea in the fall of 1931, arriving in December on the north coast of the main island, south and a little west of Manus. Earlier visitors had written that the Arapesh people who lived on the coast had a rich ceremonial life and built large, interesting triangular houses for the men. These descriptions were enough to make the Arapesh people sound like a promising culture in which to study sex roles.

When they arrived in New Guinea, however, they found that the coastal Arapesh "belonged" to the English anthropologist they had heard about in Australia, Gregory Bateson. They felt they had to

Mead's house in Alitoa. She and Reo decided to continue their study among the mountain-dwelling Arapesh.

find a different site. Some other Arapesh lived in a high plains region behind the north coastal range of the Torricelli Mountains. They decided to cross the mountains and work with the plains Arapesh. For this trip to the interior, Reo succeeded in hiring enough men and boys—fifty carriers—to pack in their supplies for six months. But bad luck seemed to be following them. The carriers left them suddenly and for no apparent reason in the village of Alitoa, on the top of the mountain. Reo could not even find them to try to convince them to continue.

Forced to Stay with Mountain Arapesh

Since they had no way to get the carriers back or find others, Reo and Margaret were forced to make the best of their situation by staying among the mountain-dwelling Arapesh in Alitoa. They began studying the language. Then disaster struck again. Margaret broke her ankle and could not move about. The women she wanted to study spent most of their time away from the village, tending their yam gardens.

The only way Mead could make use of her time was by studying the children. She began developing her theory that a culture "grew" through the learning of its children. She decided that she would describe the education and growth of the young to enliven her picture of life among the Arapesh women and society. She called this new method of writing anthro-pology "event analysis," a description of culture that placed small events in larger contexts. Once more, she was innovating.

As for her study of differences in sex roles, Mead found that among the mountain Arapesh, the roles of men and women were too similar to be useful for her study. Both men and women were gentle and nurturing in Alitoa.

Up the Yuat River

Margaret and Reo left the Arapesh people in August 1932. They both felt unhappy about the results of their stay. Tired from

Temperament of Arapesh Men and Women

Mead recounts in Blackberry Winter *the similarities in temperament between men and women in the mountain Arapesh community.*

"In Arapesh, both men and women were expected to be succoring and cherishing and equally concerned with the growth of children. Boys helped to feed . . . their small betrothed wives, and husbands and wives together observed the taboos that protected their newborn children, the whole adventure of living centered on making things grow—plants, pigs, and most of all, children. The father's role in conception was essentially a feeding role, for many acts of intercourse were believed to be necessary to build up the baby, which was compounded of father's semen and mother's blood.

Aggressive behavior—behavior that involved disregard for the rights of others and also for the rules forbidding a man to eat his own pigs, the game he killed, or the yams he grew—was heavily disapproved. And it was not the aggressor who was disapproved and punished, but anyone who roused anger and violence in another person."

In Alitoa, after deciding that the roles of women were too similar to be useful for her study, Mead concentrated on studying children. It was here that she began developing her theory that a culture "grew" through the learning of its children.

fighting malarial fever, they rested for six weeks at a plantation on the coast while they discussed finding an unwesternized site up the Sepik River, where they hoped to find some sex-role differences.

Finally they chose the Mundugumor people. Although the Mundugumor had been forced by the Australian government to give up some cultural practices, such as cannibalism, pillaging, and war, the change had happened only three years before.

The Mundugumor lived in the interior of New Guinea, south and then west up the Sepik River, on a swift tributary called the Yuat River. The Yuat was about two city blocks wide, bordered by palms and grassy banks. Canoes, called *pinnaces*, could not find anywhere to moor for as far as fifty miles. Margaret reached Kenakatem Village on the Yuat after a difficult canoe trip upriver.

Margaret and Reo found that the Mundugumor people remembered their cannibal days with pleasure. As Mead said in a letter from Kenakatem Village in September, "Boys of twelve have eaten hu-

man flesh and they show merely a mischievous and merry glee in describing their previous diet."[33] Like the Arapesh, the Mundugumor raised gardens of yams. They also hunted crocodiles and gathered crocodile eggs, which they cooked up into a kind of fritter.

The Mundugumor people, like most Oceanic cultures, practiced *avoidance taboos*. The men had their own road, closer to the river, that led to the men's "club" houses. There, wrote Mead, "they sat at ease among their kin and ate the bowls of boiled sago and fish brought there by their submissive, hard-working wives."[34] The women's roads wound through the village and around the mounds on which the people planted their coconut trees to protect them from flooding during the wet season.

While working among the Mundugumor, Margaret and Reo began to experience new tensions from illness and from disagreements about their work. Both were subject to recurrences of malaria. When Reo was sick, he treated himself

Mundugumor Temperament

While still looking for contrasts between men and women, Mead began to be more alert to the systems of expectations she could observe in Kenakatem village. She says in her autobiography that

"the Mundugumor contrasted with the Arapesh in every conceivable way. Fierce possessive men and women were the preferred type; warm and cherishing men and women were culturally disallowed. A woman who had the generosity to breastfeed another woman's infant simply did not find another husband when she was widowed. Both men and women were expected to be positively sexed and aggressive. In general, both rejected children and, where the children that were allowed to survive were concerned, adult men and women strongly favored children of the opposite sex. In Arapesh the women were kept away from the gardens for their own protection, because yams disliked anything to do with women. . . . Here again, in Mundugumor, I found a very strong cultural styling of personality, but as in Arapesh, both men and women were expected to conform to a single type: the idea of behavioral styles that differentiated men and women was wholly alien. As far as my central problem was concerned, I felt completely stalemated."

severely and went off alone. Margaret, trying to treat her fevers with quinine and rest, felt abandoned. Reo now wanted to do his own ethnography, rather than cooperating with Margaret. He wanted to describe the culture as a whole and have Margaret concentrate on the language, the children, and the technology.

And once again, in Mundugumor, Mead felt she was not making progress on her sex-role research because although there were differences between the roles of males and females, the personalities of both sexes were equally aggressive and violent. Both men and women preferred children of the opposite sex and practiced infanticide when the child was of the "wrong" sex. In fact, the children in the Mundugumor village seemed unwanted. They were not treated with respect or loving care.

As she watched the harsh treatment the children received from their parents, Margaret began to want a child, no matter how difficult that might be. She began to hope for a child she herself could nurture.

To make up for having no luck on her project, she looked for things about the Mundugumor that were pleasant. She saw that, unlike the Manus, who quarreled all the time, these villagers politely postponed their quarrels until after Margaret and Reo would leave. Their language was easy to learn. Their art was intricate and a good subject for photography. The women's grass skirts were well made and beautiful.

Their religion centered around colorful, mysterious ceremonies. After the men decorated flutes up to eight feet long with tails of animals and piles of shells and rings, they celebrated the "birth" of the flutes as if they were living beings, or gods, that could call the people together.

Meeting Bateson

Margaret celebrated her thirty-first birthday on the Yuat River. Then, before Christmas, Margaret and Reo packed and went downriver to spend the holiday at a government station. Again they sailed past the settlements of the beach-dwelling people of the Sepik River, including the village of Tambunam, with its beautiful gables and peaked ceremonial house set in a great green plaza. This interesting village was part of the culture that "belonged" to Bateson.

Nevertheless, they docked at the Iatmul village where Bateson was living and were pleasantly surprised to receive a warm welcome. The loneliness of field work brought the three anthropologists together, and from Christmas Eve until New Year's, Bateson told them about "his" people, the Iatmul. He even said he was willing to have Margaret and Reo work among some of the people he did not have time to study, since the Iatmul actually were divided into three rival groups.

Mead and Reo agreed to research a lake village called Tchambuli. Mead hoped that at last she would find a culture

Reo (middle) and Tchambuli men go to a ceremony in canoes. In Tchambuli, Mead found that women and men played almost opposite roles of those played by most cultures.

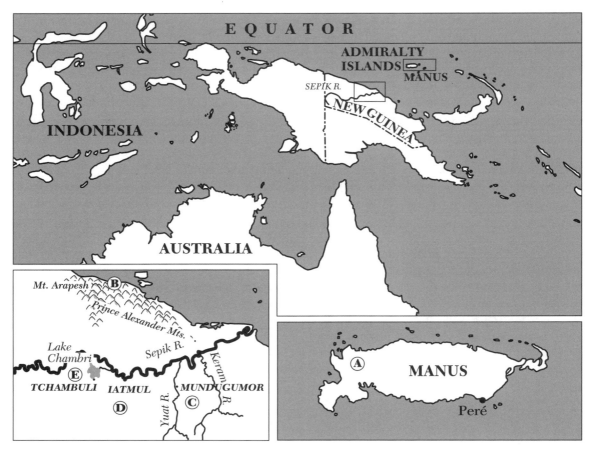

Between 1928 and 1933 Mead visited and studied five different cultures in the Pacific Islands. Her first visit was to Manus, located among the Admiralty Islands north of New Guinea (A). On her next trip she studied the mountain-dwelling Arapesh in Alitoa (B). Continuing her stay in New Guinea, Mead studied the Mundugumor along the Yuat River (C), the Iatmul along the Sepik River (D), and finally the Tchambuli, who dwell alongside Lake Chambri (E).

in which the roles of men and women were oppositional—and she did. But even more interestingly, she found patterns that developed her understanding of personality and temperament in a culture. The women in Tchambuli seemed to her more like her own (American) idea of men—outgoing, businesslike and career-oriented. The men were more like her idea of women—gossipy, primping, quar-

reling about petty things. The children took after the same-sex parents: "The little girls were as bright and competent as their mothers . . . bright and free, while the small boys were already caught up in the rivalrous, catty, and individually competitive life of the men."[35]

In this culture Mead could not feel bored. There were many things going on—almost too many to keep up with, partly because she was so tired. Bateson, unlike Reo, recognized her weariness. His sympathy gave her new energy, and in her excitement she began to exchange notes with him, carried back and forth by canoe. Mead once more began to see patterns. In her autobiography she later wrote:

> And now at last, after working in two cultures in which I had thought I was finding nothing really relevant to the problem with which I had come to the field, Tchambuli was providing a kind of pattern—in fact, the missing piece—that made possible a new interpretation of what we already knew. Very often it is only this kind of comparison of different cultures that reveals what the dimensions of a problem actually are, and so enables one to restate the problem in new terms. Contrast through comparison is necessary to complete a picture.[36]

The three anthropologists met to explore their insights into the new psychology of culture. In late-night discussions they told each other about how they fit in their own countries, Reo in New Zealand, Mead in the United States, and Bateson in England. And something else was happening to their relationship. Mead wrote in *Blackberry Winter*:

> The intensity of our discussions was heightened by the triangular situation. Gregory and I were falling in love, but this was kept firmly under control while all three of us tried to translate the intensity of our feelings into better and more perceptive field work. As we dealt with the cultural differences between Arapesh, Mundugumor, Tchambuli, and Iatmul, we talked also about the differences in temperamental emphasis in the three English-speaking cultures—American, New Zealand, and English—that we represented. . . . No part of this was irrelevant to our struggle to arrive at a new formulation of the relationships between sex, temperament, and culturally expected behavior."[37]

During her discussions with Bateson and Reo, as Mead spoke about her inner likes and dislikes, she felt she was finally stripping off her own layers of culture and finding out who she really was. The feelings she had experienced as a "misfit" at DePauw began to make anthropological sense. Temperamentally, she and Gregory were "deviants" in their materialistic cultures, she thought, while Reo fit the expectations of his male-dominated New Zealand culture. This realization led Margaret to see that, temperamentally, Reo was not the man she wanted as the father of her children. The strain would eventually prove too much for Reo and Margaret's marriage, but no one talked about such problems as the three anthropologists left New Guinea together in the spring of 1933. However, from Australia Margaret went back to her job at the museum in New York. Reo went first to New Zealand and then to England, "where he again met Eileen, the girl with whom he had originally been in love. Gregory went home to Cambridge on a freighter."[38]

5 Beautiful Bali with Gregory Bateson

Mead's field trips and collaboration with Reo proved fruiful. Her second book, *Growing Up in New Guinea*, sold as successfully as her first. Anthropologists were interested in her innovative practices. In five short years she had become a well-established writer and scientist.

She wasted no time during the winter of 1934-1935, starting immediately to write up the theories she had developed with Reo and Bateson in New Guinea. In the resulting book, *Sex and Temperament in Three Primitive Cultures*, she explained how cultures encouraged certain temperamental attitudes and behaviors, regardless of sex. Each of the cultures—Manus, Mundu-gumor, and Tchambuli—*educated* all its people to *fit* the roles assigned to men and women. According to her neat, four-directional diagram, temperaments could be characterized as "cold" or "warm," "strong" or "nurturing," and she lined them up on intersecting axes running north and south, east and west. The Arapesh and Mundugumor temperaments seemed to fit the north and south (cold and warm) poles of the scheme. The Manus fit the "east" (strong) type. Even though she wanted her formulations to be neat and symmetrical, she finished her book without the fourth type she was sure existed.

This four-way scheme of tempera-

ments was one Mead worked on for the next thirty-five years, continually looking for better ways to explain it. In a speech she gave in 1972, she explained the theory in these terms:

> We haven't any scientific reason to believe that as men and women the sexes differ in emotion. You can have a society where men weep and you can have a society where they are betrayed into weeping with forged documents. You can have a society in which it's men who perform the mourning or men who go into elaborate fits and women are quiet and controlled and do the marketing. As far as we know there are types of people that are emotional and there are male and female versions of them. There are types of people that are not emotional and there are male and female versions of them. . . . Some societies say all men and all women must be lions. Then the lord help the rabbits in either sex. Some societies say all the men and all the women are rabbits. And there have been a few societies that have said all the men are lions and all the women are rabbits. They don't have a very good time, either. When all the people are lions, they probably have an even worse time. As long as we put in the hands of

women the welfare of identified human beings, and put in the hands of men large scale organizational decisions about margin of profit, men and women will look different. And if you gave the men the personal decisions and the women the decisions on large scale margins of profit, you'd reverse the emotionality rather quickly.[39]

Other scientists attacked the neatness of Mead's scheme, but she stuck by her conclusion that science knows very little about sex differences. At least, she said, her research hinted at the ways a society molds all the men and women born within it.

The new territory she had broken would not be well understood for many years. Separated from Reo, however, Margaret headed in the direction of understanding when she accepted a pioneering invitation from another innovative thinker, Lawrence K. Frank. In the summer of 1935 she participated in his "interdisciplinary conference," which brought together professionals in psychology, politics, mental health, and physical health. At Frank's conference Mead came into close contact with experts from all these fields in an atmosphere of cooperation and competition. Mead immediately saw that she could include these concepts in her books about primitive peoples. She wrote another analysis, based on her work at the conference, of her three New Guinea cultures and called it *Cooperation and Competition Among Primitive Peoples*.

Her other book on New Guinea, *Sex and Temperament in Three Primitive Societies*, emphasized the different ways in which the behavior of men and women was stylized in the Arapesh, Mundugumor, and Tchambuli cultures. Even with—or perhaps because of—the criticism it received, the book sold well and was reprinted several times. Four of these reprintings sold thousands of copies each. Margaret considered this her most important book.

World Events Move Toward World War II

Instead of going back to New Guinea in the spring of 1935, as he had planned, Gregory Bateson came to the United States to get Margaret's help with defini-

Mead married Gregory Bateson, convinced that she had finally found a "perfect intellectual and emotional working partnership."

tions of culture, society, and cultural character for the book he was writing. Once Margaret's divorce from Reo was finalized, she and Gregory made plans to return to the South Pacific despite the threatening atmosphere field workers faced as Hitler became more prominent in Europe. Gregory and Margaret thought that by combining their studies of art, drama, and music in the country of Bali, they would find there the missing link for their temperament diagram.

They were married in Singapore and arrived in Bali on March 23, 1936, the Balinese New Year's Day. Margaret was full of hope and looked forward to cooperation in two full years of field work, for she was sure she and Gregory shared the same nurturing and industrious temperament. She expected a "perfect intellectual and emotional working partnership in which there was no pulling and hauling resulting from competing temperamental views of the world."[40]

Bali was as beautiful as they had read. Compact villages stood close together on orderly, terraced, and planted hills. Balinese people crowded the roads, energetically carrying high, heavy loads on their heads or shoulders. At almost any time of the day, Margaret could hear the music of bells or flutes or singing, or see a whole orchestra or a troop of dancers. There were dozens of rituals to observe—a ritual for every part of life from birth to death, from planting to harvest, from carving a

Mead found Bali, with its compact villages and orderly, planted hills, a beautiful place to continue her work.

Food sellers on a village street in Bajeong Gede. Here, Mead found the pace of life much slower than on the coast of Bali.

religious statue to making a serving bowl.

Since other anthropologists and artists were already studying in Bali, Mead was eager to establish some patterns of collaboration. Colin McPhee's work on houses and music in Bali would help her with that part of the Balinese culture, and Jane Belo's studies of trance would help with Mead's theories on how young children were schooled to become adults in the Balinese culture. Rhoda Métraux, who became Mead's lifelong friend, as well as her closest companion during Mead's last twenty years, was also there, working on a general ethnology.

For the first two months Margaret and Gregory studied the language with their Balinese secretary, I Madé Kaler, who knew five languages, including 18,000 words in English. As they were learning the Balinese language they studied previous descriptions of Balinese culture. Gregory studied ancient texts and dictionaries of the Balinese priests, for the Balinese had practiced writing for centuries. They found Balinese very difficult to learn because it had seventeen levels of vocabu-

lary, which were used according to strict rules of etiquette. To use any word in a sentence, they had to know which level of vocabulary to use. To do that, they also had to learn how to tell the rank and caste of both speaker and listener. Vocabulary was also very exacting in terms of meaning. For example, there were ten verbs that meant "to cut," and only one verb would be understood if Mead asked her helper to "slice" the bread.

Every day Margaret and Gregory took time off from their language studies to attend ceremonies or dances. Using their eyes and ears, as they had done when studying primitive cultures, they described every action—the cock fighting; the "offering ceremonies," in which swaying little girls in a trance were carried on the shoulders of other dancers; the shadow plays, performed when babies were born; and the weddings.

After they had learned the language, they decided to move to Bajeong Gede, a village farther inland in the mountains, hoping to find even more old-fashioned, unwesternized people there. Their house in Bajeong Gede was built especially for them and consisted of a set of cement-floored pavilions roofed with bamboo shingles and connected by shaded walks. Their furniture was made by Chinese carpenters and consisted of seventeen tables—whether they needed that many or not. Their tiny lamps burned oil inside tall glass chimneys.

They found the Bajeong mountain

Shadow Plays in Bali

In one of her Letters from the Field, *written on Christmas Eve in 1936, Mead describes the complexity of a Balinese shadow play, which was part of the ritual of accepting a newborn baby.*

"For two successive nights there were shadow plays and at midnight, when the play was over, the *dalang*, the master of the shadow play, solemnly blessed and sprinkled the [newborn] baby all over again.

These were my first shadow plays (Wajang Kulit). I had handled hundreds of the angular, grotesque puppets of painted leather as they lay uncomfortably in Museum boxes. And I had seen a model of a shadow play set up in a German museum with the puppets flat against the other side of a thin screen and the light shining through the ornamental perforations in the figures. I knew that the hands were fastened to sticks so that they could be gestured into all sorts of angular but significant positions. But I really wasn't prepared for a shadow play at all.

The lamp, instead of casting the steady dull glow of the museum model, is a great swinging lamp with a high irregular peak of flame, and to add to the uncertainty of its light the *dalang*, who sits behind it, swings it now and then. And the puppets, far from lying flat and clearcut against the screen, move hither and thither, now half-defined, now with one whole edge or only the top of a nose fluttering in the swinging light and changing distance from the screen. Figures swoop down from the top, flutter up from the corners, retreat, advance and behead each other, all in what is really a dream world of half-definition. Meanwhile the *dalang* shouts, screams, expostulates and sings, the little four-piece orchestra tinkles on and the *dalang*'s hammer bangs and bangs against his puppet box."

Mead and children of Bajeong Gede, in Balinese festival dress.

people suspicious and uncommunicative, unlike the lowlanders. In the final analysis, however, their choice was a good one because in the mountain village, the pace was much slower than on the coast. They could see the ceremonies in better detail and take more complete notes. It was almost, they thought, as if the people moved in slow motion. Eventually, Mead learned that the slow movement and thinking of the mountain people was caused by widespread thyroid disease called goiter.

In Bajeong Gede, Mead also found the bamboo fences an advantage. The Balinese people were very reserved and often would change their actions when they saw company approaching. Mead saw very different behaviors when she peeked through the bamboo branches into the yards than when she got to the gate and began to be treated as company.

The Balinese Hindu religion, with its strict rules about ritual cleanliness, contributed to Mead's educational theories. Children were taught to eat with their "clean" right hands at meals and with their left hands for snacks. Anyone who had been to a funeral or touched "dirt"

was considered "unclean" and could not enter homes. Even sitting down to an ordinary meal in a home made people unclean for some ceremonies. Still, they could eat snacks outside without worrying about taboos. Mead theorized that this practice gave people an inner sense of separation and kept them from relating closely to one another.

Margaret and Gregory worked out an intricate method of recording the various actions they saw all around them, such as mothers teasing their children into delight and then turning away from them. Margaret recorded the actions by writing notes while Gregory used the Leica and movie cameras. When they got home, Gregory developed the film and then Margaret matched her notes with them, using the notes as a script. Together they discussed the significance of how the Balinese held their fingers either tensely spread or limply hanging. Since Gregory's pictures often were close-ups that did not show the whole scene, or he might have to stop to load the camera, Margaret's notes were often needed to re-create an overall picture. For special events, they even used

Balinese Girls Perform in a Trance

In Letters from the Field 1925-1975, *Mead describes the way two young Balinese girls go into a trance during a celebration of gift offering.*

"We are all gathered . . . by a temple which is three streams away from Bajoeng. The temple is a small wooden shrine set in a fenced enclosure in the fields. The little girls . . . slipped and hurried down the steep ravines and up again, stopping now and then to lay a few little palm-leaf baskets on specially sacred spots . . . and now the offering of the Trance Dancer Club is to be made. . . .

From long wooden boxes are taken the two pairs of sacred puppets, dolls with huge headdresses and clusters of little bells on their feet. They are fastened on a long string attached to sticks with bells on top . . . young men make the sticks vibrate . . . and the dolls dance faster and more furiously. . . .

Meanwhile our two little trance dancers are brought forward—Renoe pert, self-possessed, enjoying herself, and Misi dark, stiff, dutiful and unhappy. Renoe always peeks and never falls down or gets hurt; Misi believes it all and is always tripping over things or falling off someone's shoulders. They are about nine years old. Each kneels by a pedestal and grasps the stick with both hands. As the rhythm invades their bodies, they begin to sway faster and faster to the music. The song changes and the stick is made to stamp; they fall back limp, in trance. Now they must be dressed, gold brocaded bibs hung around their necks and fantastic golden crowns placed on their heads. Sometimes the singers start singing before they are dressed and the little dancers begin to dance in their dresser's arms."

Misi and Renoe (left to right) dancing in a trance, allow the rhythm of the music to invade their bodies.

Mead and Bateson developed an intricate method of recording the numerous daily events that they observed. Mead (far right) took detailed notes of her observations, while Bateson filmed the events with a movie camera.

stopwatches both to time the event and, later, to synchronize the film with the commentary, so they did not lose the sequence of the actions.

The use of the movie camera was the most important innovation they developed in Bali. They also took many still pictures in rapid succession, using a bulk loader and a rapid winder. The stills camera allowed them to take and develop up to 1,600 exposures in a single day. With this technology, they took twelve times as many photos as they had planned on—and Mead took ten times as many notes as before, to keep up with the camera work.

A third innovation was the use of audio recording, which permitted them to record their own commentary on any sequence of events, minor or major. Watching and recording as the event went on, they were able to pinpoint important behaviors.

Mead also continued to have the children draw. In Bali the children were very

artistic and showed much imaginative power.

After ten months, when Margaret and Gregory were getting ready to move on, Margaret summarized the many activities they had witnessed among the Balinese:

> Babies I saw at birth are walking; girls married since we came will soon be mothers. New walls have been built, the temple land has been redistributed, the rice is all in rice barns and the maize in corn barns. . . . The only things that have not happened are a birth of twins and the falling down of the roof of the chief priest's house. . . . I have persuaded the little girls to draw and Sambeth has become an outstanding artist whose drawings adorn the mossy walls, cut out in relief, of practically every house in the village.[41]

Balinese Character, the book Gregory and Margaret wrote in 1938 from their film and audio records, set a new standard of accuracy and a model method in anthropology. As Margaret said later in *Blackberry Winter*, "There are still no records of human interaction that compare with those that Gregory made in Bali and then in Iatmul."[42] They obtained a record number of samples—20 birth feasts, 15 occasions when the same little girls danced in trance, 600 kitchen gods. One man painted 40 of his dreams, which could be studied in the context of 100 other artists' work.

They had worked so efficiently they felt they had learned what they needed to know to write about Balinese character. However, Margaret and Gregory both realized that they had too little comparative material to write a convincing theory about how each culture educates children to fit its requirements. They decided to travel back to the Sepik River to take comparative pictures in New Guinea.

Among the Iatmul, they thought, they would be able to use their new techniques quickly in familiar territory. But when they got there, they found that the weather was so different from that of their previous visit that the people were behaving very differently. The Sepik River area was in drought, and the men were all busy hunting crocodiles instead of staying in the village and performing ceremonies.

However, the situation offered other opportunities for comparison. During a crocodile hunt, one man was bitten by a death adder, and two children also died. Now Mead was able to observe the behavior of the Iatmul people in mourning. She saw that they treated death with deep feeling, yet with great simplicity and directness. Even small children were quiet and

Lacking enough comparative material to complete their theory, Mead and Bateson returned to the Sepik River to study the Iatmul. They are pictured here in the mosquito room of their house, where they did much of their work.

well behaved in the presence of death. No one seemed horrified by the sight or feel of a dead body. In an account included in *Letters from the Field*, Mead described Iatmul behavior after the death of a relative:

> A mother holds her dead baby in her arms, strokes it and fondles it as she would in life. . . .
>
> Mourning is almost entirely women's business. The father of a child may sit and mourn a little apart; a young mother's brother may come and sit with the women, mourning for his sister's son. But for the most part it is only women. The main mourning group, the close relatives, sit about the body, weeping loudly if it is their habit to weep loudly, otherwise quietly, while the more distantly connected come in and sit for a while in the shadowy corners of the great house floor from which all the mosquito baskets have been removed. There is a keening tune into which words are fitted, extemporaneous and almost always very simple statements of some past event: "We went together to fish, we were of one mind . . . . We were of one mind, why have you left me?"[43]

During their six-months stay in Iatmul, in addition to the setback in recording the ceremonial activities, Gregory was ill for several days. Still, they ended up with the necessary comparative material in pictures and notes. Margaret wrote in *Blackberry Winter* about the happy results of their trip:

> We could contrast the way the Balinese mother and the Iatmul mother handled a whole range of behavior—the way, for instance, the Balinese mother borrowed another baby in order to send her own child into a frenzy of

Mead, following her return to New York. By this time Mead was a famous anthropologist.

> jealousy in contrast to the way the Iatmul mother protected her child from jealousy, even as she kept her breast steady for a newborn infant which she was nursing for the first time. We could contrast the way the Balinese confined drama and action to the theater and maintained their everyday relationships placidly and evenly, never allowing children to contend even for a toy, whereas the Iatmul, who struggled and screamed and quarreled in real life, used their artistic performances to introduce moments of static beauty into their more violent lives.[44]

Crocodile Hunting on the Sepik River

This account of August 12, 1938, included in Letters from the Field 1925-1975, *describes the dry time during which Mead and Bateson revisited the Iatmul on the Sepik River in New Guinea.*

"The whole rhythm of our lives . . . is at present dependent upon the slight variations in the height of the river which mean it is or is not possible to shoot crocodiles. This is the lowest water in five years, the first time that the people have been sufficiently in the good books of their capricious shamanic spirits to be allowed to find an abundance of meat for the death feasts which will be made at high water. For hundreds of square miles land that is usually dotted with lakes . . . and itself a mere squashy quagmire, has dried up, and the people go and burn it off in great patches, laying bare the remaining sorry little puddles in which the crocodiles and turtles and fish are plunging about. Then the whole hunting group takes part in the actual crocodile hunt. They go and camp for days while this is going on and only return to the village when there is a death or a quarrel or when their supplies of worked sago runs out. . . .

The air [got] thick with smoke, for everywhere fish and the meat of crocodiles . . . were being smoked . . . a lake which had become little more than a series of mud pools in which the fishers wallowed up to their waists, first stabbing at random in the mud in the hope of hitting a fish and afterwards feeling about up to their armpits in mud to find their victims. The fish were then tossed ashore where children, up to their necks in mud, caught them and strung them on string."

At the end of 1936, Margaret and Gregory headed back to the United States, and by the time they reached New York, the world had moved close to war. But the books Mead had already written and published—*Coming of Age in Samoa, Growing Up in New Guinea,* and *Sex and Temperament in Three Primitive Cultures*—were well known and widely discussed. To her

knowledge of five Oceanic cultures two more were now added—Balinese and Iatmul. Mead thus had the raw material that would bring her to the foreground in many wartime projects and assure the continuation of her involvement both in the nation's policies and in many anthropological projects after the war was over.

Before she and Gregory became

deeply involved in wartime work, they were able to analyze miles of film and many hours of tape recordings and begin the book they would write together, *Balinese Character: A Photographic Analysis*. They obtained special grants to print this expensive, oversize book, which contained eighty full pages of six to twelve photographs each, meticulously described in captions that explained the significance of each behavior in eating, playing, dancing, relaxing, and watching each other. They were even able to make a short return trip to Bali in 1939 to clear up confusion on points they had missed.

During those last pre-war years, Mead heard about the work in child and ego development of a young psychologist, Erik Erikson. Remembering her interdisciplinary studies with Lawrence K. Frank, she enlisted Erikson's help in thinking about temperament. Erikson became a colleague with whom she would cooperate on many committees and task forces during and after the war. In this environment, the progress of Mead's career would take off from her theories of temperament and education and grow as World War II gathered force.

Mead's biographer Robert Cassidy assessed the achievement that Mead's work represented at this point. She had studied seven primitive Oceanic cultures—those of the Samoans, Manus, Arapesh, Mundugumor, Tchambuli, Iatmul, and Balinese. Cassidy writes:

> The [seven] pre-war voyages . . . can be said to comprise the foundation of Mead's anthropological research and provided the raw material for not only her major popular books, but also her lesser-known works such as *Male and Female, Cooperation and Competition Among Primitive Peoples, Continuities in Cultural Evolution,* and *Balinese Character: A Photographic Analysis* (with Gregory Bateson).[45]

These books would occupy some of Mead's time during the 1940s. But the bulk of her work would be related to the world conflict that was threatening to engulf the entire globe.

6 Motherhood and Wartime Anthropology

World War II brought both new hopes and new tensions into Margaret's life. Its opportunities for service provided her with a much broader base of fame. Writing about Bali took nearly four times as long as her other books because she and Gregory were looking at all the pictures and listening to all the tape recordings. Over and above all this, they became parents.

While working in Mundugumor, Margaret had renewed her hope to have a child. But each time she conceived, she miscarried early in pregnancy. In the winter of 1939, she once again suspected a pregnancy. Six weeks later she knew. In *Blackberry Winter*, she wrote:

> From the moment it was certain that I was pregnant, I took extreme precautions. I took a leave of absence from the Museum and gave up riding on streetcars, trains, and buses, I was given vitamin E . . . and I kept the baby.[46]

Margaret and Gregory had been planning to finish their book on Bali not in the United States, but in Cambridge, England, where Gregory held a fellowship in Trinity College. But Margaret felt that it would be dangerous to travel, given her history of miscarriages. "Now," she said in her autobiography,

it appeared that I might have to have the baby in America and cope with all the tiresome regulations of hospitals and doctors that made breast feeding difficult and prevented a mother from keeping the baby in the room with her.[47]

Instead of looking for an obstetrician, Margaret contacted a pediatrician. Dr. Benjamin Spock, a young child-development specialist, was her first choice. She thought if she could convince him about her ideas on bringing up children, he could help her find an obstetrician who would let her give birth naturally, as did women who had never even heard of hospitals.

Even though she was older—already thirty-eight—her argument convinced Dr. Spock that she could nurse the child on its own feeding schedule. At that time doctors usually recommended instead that the child be kept in the nursery and bottle-fed. Dr. Spock also agreed to allow filming of the baby's birth, so that Margaret could study what it told her about her baby's personality.

He helped her find an obstetrician, Dr. Claude Heaton, who arranged to show the sisters at New York's French Hospital some films from New Guinea. They coop-

Birth of Mead's Child

Robert Cassidy, in Margaret Mead: A Voice for the Century, *describes Catherine's birth. Mead wanted a record kept on everything she did as an anthropologist, even her private life.*

"Mead's only child was born to her and Gregory Bateson late in 1939, after the outbreak of the war. It was by no means a routine birth, for Mead had had numerous miscarriages in the course of her three marriages, and the prospective mother took no chances. The actual circumstances of the birth, told in detail in *Blackberry Winter*, were unremarkable, except that it had to be held up for ten minutes while a friend who was filming the event rushed out to her car for a flashbulb. Mead was quite insistent about having the birth filmed. She was convinced from her studies of children in Oceanic cultures that a baby exhibits certain aspects of temperament right from birth, and she wanted to know as much about her child's temperament as possible. She had also arranged to have a pediatrician present, an unheard of practice at the time. The young doctor, Benjamin Spock (who would go on to worldwide fame as the author of *Baby and Child Care*), managed to find a hospital that would comply with Mead's request that no anesthetic be administered and that she be allowed to nurse the baby on demand. The nursing sisters at New York's French Hospital took it all in stride and so, happily, did the baby, Mary Catherine. "

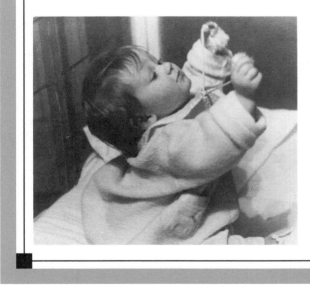

Infant Mary Catherine.

erated with her wish to breastfeed the baby whenever it was hungry and not to use an anesthetic unless it was absolutely necessary.

Margaret and Gregory spent the summer months cataloging their 25,000 Balinese pictures, which were still on long strips of film and had to be held up to the light to be identified. Mead also taught a class on parenting in other cultures for the Child Development Department at Vassar College.

She consulted regularly with the physicians and psychologists there about her health and the baby's development, and stayed on a low-calorie diet of vegetables. While she knitted for the baby, she thought about her new role, that of modeling for American women how they could choose values from different cultures for the good of their babies. She worried that the child might inherit deafness, a family trait. She stayed open to having either a boy or a girl, and she determined "not to limit the child that was to be born—not to hope for it to be beautiful or intellectually gifted or temperamentally happy."[48]

In August, Gregory was called home to England. Margaret lived with her college classmate, Marie Eichelberger, for the three months he was to be away. Much in demand to accept honors and give speeches about Samoa and New Guinea, she gave the Seventy-fifth Anniversary Address at her alma mater, Barnard College, in October.

On December 7 she was continuing her work on the Balinese films when she received a cable from Gregory saying that he was applying for a permit to come to America. On December 8 her father came for a visit and they went out for supper. Within a few minutes after returning to her apartment, she knew that she had gone into labor and needed to call the hospital.

At the hospital she timed her own labor pains and considered the irony of men thinking that they needed to teach women that childbearing is natural. As she had requested, she took no pain-killers. The baby—a normal, healthy, seven-pound girl—was born without complications on December 8, 1939, and the whole

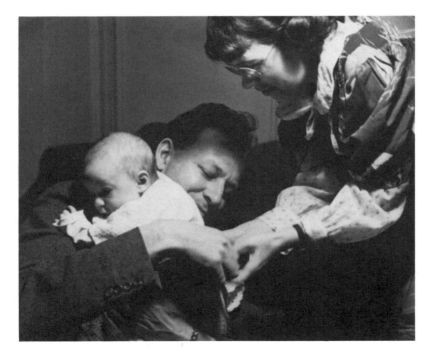

On December 8, 1939, while Bateson was in England, Mead gave birth to a healthy baby girl, Mary Catherine. Bateson, the proud father, soon returned home to be with his newborn daughter.

procedure was filmed by Myrtle McGraw. The nurses brought Margaret the baby every three hours and let her keep it in her room through the night.

Parenting for the Two Anthropologists

Gregory was still in England, but Margaret and he had discussed the child's name before he had left—it could not be William if it was a boy, because the Batesons already had too many famous Williams. If it was a girl, it would be named Mary, after Gregory's aunt, and Catherine, after the sister Margaret had named (but spelled with a *C* to match the initials of Gregory's mother). Thus, both the relatives after whom Mary Catherine was named were people who had died young. Margaret liked to think of this as "a promise that an interrupted pattern will, after all, be completed."[49] Like Margaret, Gregory intended to treat Mary Catherine as "a separate person with an identity completely her own."[50] When she was three days old, she received from her father a package addressed to "Miss Mary Catherine Bateson."

Margaret wanted to document and record Mary Catherine's life just as she had done for her sisters, Priscilla and Elizabeth, and for children of other cultures. Notes helped her to collaborate with Dr. Spock and professionals in mental health and education to raise Catherine with all of the newest scientific ideas. And as she said later in *Blackberry Winter*, she had

> many friends . . . from circles in which children were a major preoccupation—educators, child analysts, and

Bateson plays with daughter Catherine. Like Mead, Bateson encouraged their daughter's independence.

child psychologists. They all shared my delight in having a child. And so did my childless friends—Jane Belo, who had been so close to us in Bali and who had been with us in Kintamani when I lost a baby there, and Marie Eichelberger, who took Cathy as her special charge and became "Aunt Marie" forever.[51]

Notes would help her to watch Catherine for answers to the question that had fascinated her in her research: What roles do culture and heredity play in child development? She felt she could find the answer by watching her own child, keeping in mind her own ancestral biology and her American culture.

She tried never to show any negative reactions, no matter what Catherine did, for she had seen in the field, especially in Bali, how sensitive children are to their

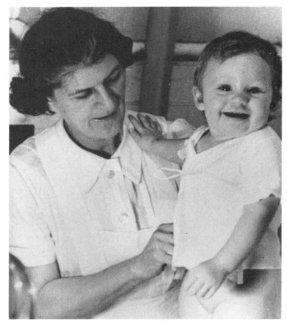

Catherine with Helen Burrows, 1940. Burrows was a patient and devoted nanny who helped raise Catherine while Mead was working.

parents' emotional responses. She did not want to handicap her child by negative responses that could be interpreted as heredity. She reasoned in *Blackberry Winter*:

> The traits in which one takes pride and the traits of the other parent whom one loves are doubly endearing in the shared child. The child who is born with such a combination, as I was, starts off in life with a special blessing. But the child who displays repudiated [rejected] parental traits starts life with a handicap. The parents have to make an extra effort not to respond negatively to those traits in their child which they dislike or fear in themselves.[52]

Margaret preferred to raise Catherine in the affectionate and nurturing way she had seen among the Samoans, the mountain Arapesh, and the Manus people rather than the harsh and spartan upbringing she had observed among the Mundugumor. Yet, she knew her career would not allow for continuous, intense contact. For the times that her work would take her out of the home she hired a British widow, Helen Burrows, who had a fourteen-year-old daughter, Audrey, to be Catherine's nanny. Helen was devoted to Cathy and patient in bringing up the baby.

Helping with the War Effort

Meantime, the world was deeply embroiled in World War II. The Allied nations were looking for anthropologists to become advisers to the government. Bateson was hired by the American government to tell them what he knew about the people of the South Pacific, where tension with Japan was building up. He was also called to Washington, D.C., to share his special understanding of the British.

The U.S. government also asked Mead and Ruth Benedict to use their knowledge of cultures to help the war effort. Ruth joined the Office of Strategic Services in Washington, D.C. Mead went to England in 1941 to give talks on American culture to the British, to help the two Allied countries understand each other and work together. She traveled in England for more than six months to speak to radio audiences, women's clubs, parents' groups, and members of the armed forces about the way Americans differed from the British in their attitudes toward women and work. She said that when Americans joined together as partners, they thought the important goal was either to focus on their own expertise—what they knew best how to do—or to contribute what they had, their know-how or their money. On the other hand, she said, the British considered partnership to be an equal sharing of burdens—a sharing that had little to do with what the individuals had to contribute.

When Mead returned home in the fall of 1941, she toured the United States to give speeches, taking notes continually on the similarities and differences she saw between the British and the Americans. These experiences in speaking before British and American audiences gave her the material for her book on wartime morale, *And Keep Your Powder Dry*, published in 1942.

This book described the American character in the same style as her books about Samoa and New Guinea. Its purpose was to help Americans understand themselves so that they could continue supporting the soldiers who were giving their lives on the front lines, and successfully receive the men back after they had lived in other cultures. She reminded people that after the end of the war, the warring nations would need to live and work together again. Underneath, all people were alike; it was their cultures that brought about their feelings of difference, and consequently of fear and distrust.

Influence of Mead's Child Rearing

Years later, Margaret's daughter Cathy wrote about her own memories of life with her parents in With a Daughter's Eye.

"Margaret's ideas influenced the rearing of countless children, not only through her own writings but through the writings of Benjamin Spock, who was my pediatrician and for whom I was the first breast-fed and 'self-demand' baby he had encountered. If the weight of early experience is as great as we believe it to be, I belong to a generation that is chronologically some five years younger than I, psychologically one of the postwar babies although I was born in 1939. . . .

Spock was blessedly relaxed about letting my mother do as she wanted, abandoning the fixed schedules that were regarded as essential to health, but he seems to have been only partly aware of the innovation taking place in front of his eyes, for he wrote later that the first experiment in 'self-demand feeding' took place in 1942, an example of the limited willingness of physicians to learn from patients."

She pointed out the strengths and weaknesses of the American character, using insights from her studies of Oceanic cultures to explain how American families worked. To encourage Americans to pay attention to her suggestions, she said she could speak as an expert because she brought the special perception of an anthropologist to her observations. Her experience in the field, she said, gave her special powers of observation.

She concluded in *And Keep Your Power Dry* that Americans had enough competitiveness and strength of character to put up with rationing of sugar, meat, and gasoline. The book, like her other books, became a best-seller, and more and more groups and organizations asked her to give morale-building speeches.

As she went about the country speaking about the American family and the war effort, Mead thought of herself as having credibility because she was an anthropologist. To show how anthropologists looked at things, she often quoted this section from her book's introduction:

> Speaking from a platform to a women's club, if one is merely an experienced speaker at women's clubs, one notices whether an audience is smartly dressed, and how smartly. If one is an American sociologist, one may add observations about the probable class level of the audience and the proportion of professional women—lawyers in sober suits seeking to tone down their sex, social workers in pleasant but serviceable headgear, civil servants with clothes that look like uniforms or clothes that aggressively do *not* look like uniforms. But I never completely lose a still further point of reference—

the awareness that my audience wears clothes. [53]

During her work for the government, Mead realized that she could compare modern Americans with the people of Mundugumor and Iatmul. Mead's excitement with this insight caught on, and so strongly, that in 1942 she and Gregory, along with Ruth Benedict and Lawrence K. Frank, formed a small, volunteer organization, which they called the Council for Intercultural Relations. The council later changed its name to the Institute for Intercultural Studies (IIC) and had a specific aim:

> to create a climate of opinion of the importance of the cultural approach, to facilitate informal relationships between students of national character, to prepare and distribute reprints for those interested in developing or applying the cultural approach to contemporary international problems, to develop new research and new research methods and to apply the cultural approach to problems of intercultural adjustment between and within nations. [54]

This organization became the power behind the group's research on the "national character" of the French, Germans, and Soviets, which they eventually called Culture at a Distance. Mead donated thousands of dollars to the IIC and convinced others to do the same. Hardly anything was recorded on how this influential group helped the war effort. Much of their activity during the war was apparently classified, but after the war they worked with the United Nations in forming UNESCO (United Nations Educational,

Catherine, Mary Frank, and her son Colin (left to right). The Franks provided a family environment for Catherine while her parents were gone.

Scientific, and Cultural Organization) and the concept of Non-Governmental Organizations (NGOs).

On Pearl Harbor Day, December 7, 1942, when Cathy was three, the government called on Mead for even more of her time and expertise. The Office of Strategic Services asked Ruth Benedict to recruit Mead for the Committee on Food Habits of the National Research Council. In addition, by the spring of 1943, Mead was called to work as executive secretary for a special nutrition committee in the Department of Agriculture, and she knew she would be spending even more time away from New York. She worked out an agreement with Lawrence Frank and his wife, Mary, to give Cathy the kind of extended family so often found in the South Pacific. Margaret, Cathy, and the Frank family all moved to New York City and lived in the Franks' large house on Perry Street. Larry had five children by former marriages. He and Mary also had an infant son, Colin. For Cathy it was like having a baby brother and five aunts and uncles, an extra pair of grandparents, and a great aunt—but often enough, no mother or father.

Mead, however, considered this large household ideal for Cathy while she commuted to Washington during the week and came to New York on weekends. Gregory was working in New York at the Museum of Modern Art, so Cathy spent weekday time with him and weekend time with Margaret, and only rarely with both parents together. Margaret longed for two uninterrupted days to spend with Cathy. When she was able to do this, she liked to brush Cathy's curly hair and try to get her to cooperate by asking her whether a tangle seemed like an elephant or a giraffe.

Then Gregory was sent to the South Pacific from February of 1944 until the end of the war, to help with psychological

Mead's Manual on Food Habits

In her preface Mead introduces the purpose of Cultural Patterns and Technical Change, *the manual of technical change that made world hunger an international byword.*

"A manual on how to introduce a new food crop, a new system of public health, a new system of wage labor into some remote part of Africa or Asia, is of significance to the man in the street in New York or London, Topeka or Coventry, Vancouver or Wellington or Brisbane. He himself will not, in ninety-nine cases out of a hundred, come close to the problem of the people in a faraway village who prefer to sleep on the ground and so are afraid of hospital beds, or who fear to sleep with others over their heads and so are afraid of two-story hospital buildings. Yet this book is about problems just like these: How does the expert member of an international technical assistance team bring to a people the help they have asked for? How can the new changes be introduced with least hazard to the mental health of those who make them? These are minutiae of expert skills which the average reader will not have to exercise—in Southeast Asia. They are nevertheless relevant to him—in two ways.

As a member of a modern nation, he faces every day changes of the same kind as those with which the expert is dealing in Burma or Iraq—the same in kind, although different in pace. We all live in a world which is being transformed before our eyes by new inventions, new forms of communication. Attention to the more dramatic instances in which the culture of a people is transformed sharpens our realization of what is happening to us.

But more urgently, we live in a world which is so haunted by the destructive powers which have been released in the twentieth century that it is of vital importance that we have reason for faith in our world. . . . Upon our ability to hope will depend our willingness to act in the living present . . . to think about the question, *How can technical change be introduced with such regard for the culture pattern that human values are preserved?* It is necessary to think about these patterns, these changes, and these considered attempts to protect the mental health of a world population in transition."

Hiroshima after the explosion of the first atom bomb. This solution to end the war, which conflicted strongly with her beliefs, had a profound impact on Mead.

warfare—radio broadcasts intended to undermine the morale of people supporting the Japanese.

At last, the explosion of the atomic bomb over Hiroshima, Japan, on August 6, 1945, ended World War II. But the solution was so drastic and went so strongly against Mead's deepest beliefs that it also changed her grasp on the future. She said, "At that point I tore up every page of a book I had nearly finished. Every sentence was out of date. We had entered a new age."[55]

7 Ambassador-at-Large, 1945-1953

Two important developments in Mead's life had taken place during her wartime travel and lectures. Her fame broadened—almost everyone in the United States, lay people as well as anthropologists and university professors, recognized her name and theories. Also, she became convinced that her knowledge and expertise could help the people of the whole world. She began to take advantage of every opportunity to give speeches, write articles, arrange seminars, and accept offices in prestigious organizations, awards for her various accomplishments, or honorary degrees from colleges and universities. As she looked at it, the fame and acclaim that was coming to her was both a gift to the world and the result of an upbringing by parents who accepted her and gave her a respect for people of every kind.

Working for Children of the World

Mead's first priority, as in her field studies, was children. She saw herself as a self-appointed ambassador-at-large for children's needs and issues. As the United Nations (UN) Charter came closer to its signing in

San Francisco in June of 1945, Mead used her growing influence to show that children were the first of the hungry people of the world to suffer. As countries recovered from war, she said, children should receive special attention and special education so that they would grow up wanting international cooperation and world peace. She was particularly proud of being a member of the three influential committees—the IIC, the Committee on Living Habits, and the World Federation on Mental Health—that evolved into the United Nations Educational, Social, and Cultural Organization (UNESCO).

As one of UNESCO's founders, Mead shaped its spirit and kept the organization focused on the educational and social needs of children. After the war and during the first years of the United Nations, Mead became concerned with the needs of developing peoples all over the world. She planned and arranged a survey to discover what kinds of help developed countries were interested in providing for underdeveloped nations. She convinced UNESCO that the information gathered should be given to "experts, policy-makers, specialists, technicians of all sorts, chiefs of missions and teams, members of ministries of health, education, agricultural and industrial development in countries actively seeking to guide technological change."[56]

Several years later, in 1952, she edited and wrote the introduction for the detailed manual that resulted from this survey, guidelines for experts who were helping the economic recovery of war-torn or undeveloped countries. UNESCO and the Federation of Mental Health were delighted to publish the manual, called *Cultural Patterns and Technical Change.*

Mead's call for wealthy nations to share food with poorer nations came out of her work with children. In 1942, following up her observations of the traders of Manus, she became interested in educating people from developed cultures about nutrition and foods from other cultures. She had explained to the national director of Extension Services for the U. S. Department of Agriculture how the public should understand how their own shopping habits affected farmers. For example, she said, they should realize that if they would not eat cheese, the farmers would sell off their dairy herds. After she initiated the idea of food education, the U.S. Department of Agriculture asked her to help establish the National Committee on Food Habits. This committee set up experiments on changing food habits for better nutrition. For example, U.S. farmers had

---

Working for the U.S. Government

Jane Howard, in Margaret Mead: A Life, *tells how "Mead's unswerving campaign to make her name and voice ever more public," rewarded her with money for the Institute for Intercultural Studies, her project of "creating a generally favorable attitude toward anthropological work on other modern cultures and demand for more work of the same kind."*

"Mead and Benedict had in mind a specific scheme for postwar study of what they now began to call "cultures at a distance" and "contemporary cultures." The Office of Naval Research granted $100,000 to finance the study, which was based first at Columbia University and later at the American Museum of Natural History, and which would give anthropologists their biggest chance yet to relate what they knew to the needs of the government. The government, they thought, had been making shamefully little use of what they had to say about who America's future enemies might be, how to break down those enemies' morale and will to fight, and how to turn enmity into good will. This new project aimed to 'develop a series of systematic understandings of the great contemporary cultures,' as Mead said, 'so that the value of each may be orchestrated in a world built anew.'"

extra tomatoes during the war; the committee helped decide where this extra food could be sent. Many of her wartime conferences and seminars had been given for the National Committee on Food Habits. By 1952, Mead had made food for hungry people a priority.

Catherine Is Growing Up

All during the war, when Mead was commuting to Washington, D.C., and traveling about the country giving lectures on the war effort, she and Cathy kept their home base in New York with the Franks. Until she was six years old and started school, Cathy often accompanied her mother to lecture halls and enjoyed special times with her, going to the zoo or playing games.

Parenting Cathy after she started school was more and more a task either Margaret or Gregory did separately and in their individual ways. After the war, soon after Gregory came home from his psychological-warfare work in the Pacific, he was called to San Francisco for months at a time to work on electronics research. During vacations or for parts of the summers, Cathy traveled between her father's apartment in San Francisco and Cloverly, New Hampshire, where the Franks lived near a community of social scientists. Catherine later wrote in *With a Daughter's Eye*:

> I spent months each summer at Cloverly while my mother came and went, spending her days in conversation with Larry or typing in a small cabin by the lake shore just remote enough from the landing to allow undisturbed work. The pattern of life in those presuburban days, if one could afford it, was to live in the city

Despite a busy schedule that frequently kept her from home in New York, Mead and Catherine enjoyed many special times together.

Margaret's Letting-Go Poem for Cathy

In January 1947, when Catherine was seven, Margaret wrote a poem to say that she did not want to haunt her daughter with her own expectations. She included the poem in Blackberry Winter.

"That I be not a restless ghost
Who haunts your footsteps as they pass
Beyond the point where you have left
Me standing in the newsprung grass,

You must be free to take a path
Whose end I feel no need to know,
No irking fever to be sure
You went where I would have you go.

Those who would fence the future in
Between two walls of well-laid stones
But lay a ghost walk for themselves,
A dreary walk for dusty bones.

So you can go without regret
Away from this familiar land,
Leaving your kiss upon my hair
And all the future in your hands."

and then go away in the summer from the heat and the polio epidemics. Every year there was a major hegira [movement of large groups of people], with an eight-hour journey by train, broken by a change in Boston.[57]

Margaret and Gregory were working together on scientific issues, but their personal lives were drifting apart. In 1949, when Catherine was ten, Gregory moved permanently to San Francisco. As an adult, Catherine remained sympathetic to her parents' personal struggles and wrote about a controlling streak she could see in her mother's personality that clashed with her father's easygoing attitudes. Even when Margaret thought she was trying to relate to Gregory's needs, Catherine said, her "efforts to accommodate the transitions in Gregory's life seemed to him a continuing effort to dominate and manipulate."[58]

A New Book

Margaret refused to indulge in self-pity when Gregory moved out. She used her field notes on Oceanic cultures to write another book, *Male and Female*, which was published in 1949. This book combined her insights on Pacific cultures, her theories of sex education, and her understanding of temperament.

She was determined to prove that

Mead's book, Male and Female, *challenged the theories of the famous psychiatrist, Sigmund Freud.*

there was a clear difference between people's temperaments and their biological sex. Using the schema of temperaments that she and Gregory and Reo Fortune had discussed in 1934 in New Guinea, she strengthened her argument that culture, or society, caused both women and men to suffer when it expected each sex to have one kind of temperament—such as aggressive or unemotional, or retiring and motherly.

Male and Female also questioned the theories of the famous psychiatrist, Sigmund Freud, about men and women. Mead especially challenged Freud's conclusion that women always envied and wanted to be like men. He had probably come to

this conclusion, Mead said, because he had not known about the different male and female roles in cultures other than his own. Women in Western cultures envied men only because women's roles were so restricted. Mead believed knowledge of other cultures proved Freud's theories wrong. Through understanding cultures such as those of the Arapesh, the Mundugumor, the Iatmul, and the Balinese, people could clearly see, she insisted, that sex roles were not biological. Instead, they often resulted from practical circumstances—for example, whether crocodiles or pigs were used for meat, whether gardens were maintained by cutting down trees or pulling weeds by hand, and whether the local temperature meant that food had to be eaten immediately rather than stored.

Male and Female also showed how Mead's educational interests had broadened through her interdisciplinary work with Larry Frank in mental health. As Mead saw it, mental health was simply another name for lack of stress and tension. Children who grew up sullen and rebellious and at odds with their parents, as adolescents in the United States often did, were not mentally healthy. When Mead wrote *Coming of Age in Samoa*, she had tried to show that Samoan adolescents were happier because their parents did not give them so many rules; therefore, they were in better mental health than adolescents in the United States. Now, in *Male and Female*, she asked questions about marriage and divorce—was it good for the children? Or could partners avoid separation by rethinking their sex roles in the marriage? *Male and Female*, as much as any other book published in the 1940s, helped to create a climate of opinion in which Americans could talk about women's ca-

Male and Female Suggests Answers

Mead's biographer, Jane Howard, quotes Mead's introduction to Male and Female, *and then comments on enthusiasm for it.*

"The new ballet between the sexes no longer follows traditional lines [but is instead] a ballet in which each couple must make up their steps as they go along. When he is insistent, should she yield, and how much? When she is demanding, should he resist, and how firmly? Who takes the next step forward or the next step back? What is it to be a man? What is it to be a woman?

These questions served to widen her already considerable audience. She could not answer them, of course, but her flair for stating them so succinctly made them seem less threatening. More and more her name took on mythological overtones: Just think, people would say, even the great Margaret Mead has these matters on her mind! It was harder to be married in America, Margaret Mead said, then anywhere else, and if she said it, it must be so. Who would know better? Her happily alliterative name was becoming more and more a synonym for fresh common sense."

reers and divorce. The book came out before Margaret and Gregory were actually divorced.

A Trip with Cathy

By 1952 Mead had finished most of the food studies, as well as cultural studies on the Soviet Union and France, all of which had been closely related to recovery from the war. This work had demanded exceedingly long hours, much travel, and intense meetings. It became more clear, in these years of estrangement and finally divorce from Gregory, that Margaret was hiding her pain by adhering to a grueling work schedule. At her office in the museum, Mead needed many students and secretaries and assistants to help with all her projects. She became known as an exacting and even tyrannical supervisor. Still, her reputation in anthropology was so great that many graduate students and museum interns wanted to work with her. They knew how much they would be able to learn from a person with her wide experience, and if they needed research money, her name opened doors.

In 1952 she had an opportunity that gave her a break in her routine. The Australian Broadcasting System invited her to Australia to give an all-expenses-paid, month-long series of lectures. Cathy, who was twelve, went along and was enrolled in the Frensham School in New South Wales, Australia, so she could share this intercultural experience. In Australia, Mead "toured the continent, delighting audiences, beginning new friendships and renewing old ones,"[59] especially the anthropologists she had met when she was married to Reo Fortune. She took a side trip to visit him and his family in New Zealand.

Some Exciting News About Manus

While in Australia Mead heard that the people of Manus, New Guinea, had begun an extraordinary cultural experiment.

The news was that they had abruptly given up their ways and, under a charismatic leader, had dived headfirst into the twentieth century.

Mead had not really wanted to return to visit the people she had studied before the war. She was afraid it would sadden her too much to find that they had lost their own native culture and become demoralized. But she heard that the Manus were different. She decided to return to New Guinea, to find out for herself what had happened there.

To ensure that the study of the Manus's cultural change would be done thoroughly, she searched for a graduate student who could help her and then continue on in New Guinea after she returned to the museum. The assistant had to be qualified in linguistics, in photogra-

New Peré Village, built ashore. Mead decided to return to Manus after learning of the drastic changes that the island people had undertaken.

Mead in her Manus house in 1953, working with an audience of young girls. Mead was amazed to find that so many changes in the culture had taken place, including the behavior of the young.

phy, and (so that he could repair radios, cameras, generators, and tape recorders) in theoretical and applied electronics. The most important qualification, however, was an interest in culture, psychology, and personality studies.

Ted Schwartz was the only qualified student who applied. His wife, Lenora, an artist, also wanted to do field work. Mead took a year to train the Schwartzes to look for the cultural patterns she was interested in, teach them the language, and experiment with cameras and tape-recording techniques.

Back to Manus, New Guinea

Mead obtained a grant for the American Museum of Natural History from the Rockefeller Foundation to fund the expedition to the Admiralty Islands for this restudy of the Manus. Her project was to record the impact of the drastic, rapid change that had taken place in less than

one generation. Mead especially wanted to interview Paliau, the New Guinea leader who had led the change. This truly historic field trip took place from July to December of 1953.

When she arrived, Mead found that everything in Peré Village had changed. Even the houses were no longer built on stilts offshore in the water. Instead, they were neatly arranged in streets along the shoreline. In fact, the entire culture had been remade. No sooner had the anthropologists arrived than they were given an extraordinary opportunity to find out in an intimate setting how the people had come through these changes. A new volcano was smoking, they were told, and the entire village of 250 people was ordered to evacuate and move to higher ground, where they could camp safely beyond the reach of a tidal wave.

Mead immediately saw that people behaved very differently from the way they had in 1936. Instead of coldness between married couples, she saw friendliness and intimacy. She wrote in a letter, published later in *Letters from the Field 1925-1975*, that

the whole group moved together with no shouting or panic and not a child cried, although usually the air is rent with the insistent screams of young children, rhythmic, stylized proclamations of their rights and wishes. But in the moment of action, waked from sleep, bundled into canoes, they were quiet and intent. Now they have made themselves at home in small spaces comparable to the platform of a canoe at sea, with small carefully watched fires on bits of galvanized iron or broken pots, and in small family groups they sit, sleep, cook, smoke, chatter, play with the babies and wait.[60]

Mead knew right away that this change, which had begun only seven years earlier in 1946, had been good for the village and was something that would "make one proud of the human race."[61]

By Saturday the volcano was declared safe, and the fleet of canoes rowed back to the village. Mead was able to take notes on three weddings. In these celebrations, she saw that the change had freed the people of Manus from the old taboos that had forbidden any show of affection between married people. Now, she saw how

each young couple, free to talk together, eat together, go about together in public, freed of all the old irksome taboos and exploitation, can sit down comfortably in a section of the house which is their very own.[62]

She met Paliau, the leader, and judged him to be both a careful planner and a skillful negotiator who had helped the people themselves work for change. His success as a politician was the result of a combination of fortunate circumstances—his close acquaintance with several Manus villages; his varied work as a laborer, a cook, and a police boy [native policeman]; his experience in a police-boy's strike; and his appointment, during the Japanese occupation, as overseer of several thousand farm workers on the island of New Britain.

By the end of the first week Mead approved of the changes in Manus. It seemed to her that there had been a kind of gentle and moving spiritual change—a bloodless, nonviolent revolution. The local organizations were continuing but with more force. The whole society worked as a unit in an orderly, yet personal way. To her, Peré Village was a microcosm (little world) of what ought to happen whenever

Mead found that the Manus babies and children were much calmer than she had observed on her previous trip.

Paliau (right) was the force behind the amazing changes that had taken place on Manus. Mead found him to be an excellent planner and negotiator, and was pleased with the island's transformation.

less advanced cultures were learning new ways. She could hardly wait to write up this success story.

Before she left, in October of 1953, she realized that everything was not perfect. The schoolteacher lacked education. Many of the supplies the people were using for their new-style houses, such as plywood, were wearing out and had to be imported at great cost. But Mead was hopeful, nonetheless. She took time to work with the teacher, helping plan some lessons for the children. In one lesson, she had the children climb a palm tree to see a map of their village drawn in the sand, their first acquaintance with maps. In a letter, she commented:

> I have to combine helping with the school with getting work done. Now . . . we have a dating scale, showing evolutionary time, time since the birth of Christ, the discovery of America, Australia and New Guinea, the two

world wars and the beginning of the new era, 1946, so they can learn, as people become literate, how to borrow a time scale from those who became literate earlier. And to make this real, all the decades since 1890 are identified with the birth of someone in the village.[63]

In December Mead left Ted and Lenora Schwartz in Manus to complete the studies while she returned to the United States and her work at the museum. Her book about her field trip, *New Lives for Old: Cultural Transformation—Manus 1928-1953* was published a little over two years later and became another best-seller. In telling the story of the Manus's remarkable change from a primitive culture to a modern one, Mead offered to the world ideas for policies that would assist other emerging cultures to make equally momentous transitions.

8 Museum Work and Increasing Recognition

From Manus, Mead went home to New York and her tower office at the American Museum of Natural History. Her job there was the most stable part of her life, most of which was spent touring, lecturing, and moving from place to place. She still had the same job she had interviewed for before she went to Samoa almost thirty years earlier—though she had been promoted from assistant to associate curator. She had helped to write her own job description, for she had taken this position at a time when museum personnel and anthropologists were evolving from collectors to educators with the responsibility of developing theories through research.

Mead's job at the museum included setting up exhibits to educate people about her field trips. She was now engaged in an even more ambitious project—preparing an entire new section of the museum, called the Hall of the Peoples of the Pacific. The project took many years, because it entailed many tasks. First, as a curator (caretaker) Mead had to ensure the preservation of the artifacts she had collected, catalogue and index them, and prepare a suitable storage place. As a scientist, she had to provide a clear picture of each new artifact's significance. As an educator, she had to present a unified picture of a whole culture through diora-

mas and rooms that explained how the culture worked, what made it unique, what particular contrasts would be interesting to museum visitors—students, schoolchildren, and their families. Finally, to get people to come to the museum to learn, she wrote up her field notes in a book, in pamphlets, and in articles for magazines such as *Redbook*, a women's magazine with a very large circulation.

Mead, with examples of Manus art brought home for the American Museum of Natural History.

Catherine Accompanies Her Mother to Israel

As she had all her life, Mead worked simultaneously on many tasks, her museum job only one of them. After the war, Mead had become involved in the formation of the state of Israel. In 1956 she was invited to Israel to be a consultant on immigration policies for the many cultural groups from Germany, Russia, China, the United States, and many other places that were gathering in the new country.

Thinking that the trip would also be an educational opportunity for Catherine, then a junior in high school, she took her daughter along. Catherine was already thinking about college, possibly at her father's place of research, Cambridge, Eng-

Catherine Finds Her Own Way in Israel

In With a Daughter's Eye, *Mary Catherine Bateson recalls touring Israel while her mother was on assignment in Tel Aviv. She felt a sense of freedom in leaving Margaret a message in Hebrew, the language of Israel:*

"After ten days I tried to reach Margaret in Tel Aviv by phone and then dictated a message for her to a hotel desk clerk in the half dozen words of Hebrew that I had picked up (but could not have written), '*Shalom, Ima, ani biyrushaleyim,*' 'Hello, Mummy, I am in Jerusalem.' When she came, the next clerk on duty, knowing who she was looked at the message and said it must be a mistake, but Margaret persisted, saying she was expecting a message from her daughter. . . . And a week later, the day before her own departure, we settled the decision for me to stay in Israel, where I learned Hebrew, entered a Hebrew high school, and received an Israeli matriculation, returning to the United States a year later to begin college.

I never lived with my mother again. I do not believe it is possible to make sense of the words I write about my parents or the ways in which I was close to them in later years without a sense of that decisive departure and separation. A quarter century later, I feel my facial muscles irresistibly shaped in a gleeful grin as I think of that telephone message and the sense of cleverness and independence it gave me, the message 'Already I am at home here and beyond your ken.' A quarter century later, I can pause and look at her achievement in letting me stay, the swiftness and the respect."

land. Both Margaret and Catherine believed that travel would broaden her education. For the two weeks they were to be in Israel, Margaret arranged for Catherine to see the country while she herself consulted with the officials in Tel Aviv.

In *With a Daughter's Eye*, Catherine tells how she appreciated the fact that her mother trusted her to travel alone and find her way in a foreign country:

> In the summer of 1956 I went with Margaret to Israel where she had been invited as a consultant on the assimilation of immigrants from different cultural backgrounds, particularly Oriental Jews, an opportunity to look at the contrast between real cultural disparity and the symbolic expression of unity. Young people were found for me to spend time with and I was soon traveling with them around the country, visiting kibbutzim [communes] of different types and listening to passages from the Old Testament and from modern Hebrew poetry.[64]

Before her mother had even finished her work, Catherine had decided she wanted to finish her high-school education in Israel. Margaret was true to her commitment to "let her be free to choose her own path."[65]

The Pain of Separation

So in 1956, after balancing parenting with her career for sixteen years, Margaret came home to New York alone. Her ever-more-demanding work at the museum helped her to cope with the pain of separation.

In particular, Mead threw her efforts into a painstaking review of the entire field of Oceanic research for the new Hall of the Peoples of the Pacific, which took another fourteen years to complete.

She also accepted several academic positions and awards. In 1957, she took a position as visiting professor of anthropology in the department of psychiatry at the University of Cincinnati College of Medicine. She taught there until 1972. She became a member of the Board of Directors of the American Association for the Advancement of Science in 1955 and remained in that position for seven years. She was appointed Sloan Professor at the Menninger School of Psychiatry in Topeka, Kansas, in 1959 and gave annual lectures there until her death.

Writing Projects

As she had all her life, Mead continued to write. She prepared the manuscript for *People and Places*, published in 1959. While the book mostly reviewed previously published material about her seven Oceanic cultures, it presented it in a new format, to an unsophisticated audience.

In addition, she collaborated with Lawrence K. (Larry) Frank on a series of articles aimed at popularizing the understanding of mental health. Among the ideas in these articles were three important ideas: that mental health had international implications, because unhappy people would revolt or fail in their national efforts; that personality could be better understood if researchers would study happy and sad people in different cultures; and that the field of mental health was changing because of women's liberation.

Mead's fame brought increased recognition to the museum's research program. In 1957 the museum sent her back to Bali to record the changes that had taken place there since her first visit in 1936.

Such writing for a wide audience brought her even more listeners and increased her sphere of influence so that people began to ask her opinion on almost every issue. She wrote and published articles on questions about women and on adolescent education in different cultures. As a reflection of her knowledge and understanding of issues related to mental health, she was asked to serve as president of the World Federation for Mental Health from 1956 to 1957.

The museum's research program continued to benefit from her reputation as an anthropologist. Since *New Lives for Old*, her restudy of Manus, had been so successful, the museum sent her back to Bali to record the changes that had taken place there since her first visit in 1936.

Mead's Increasing Fame

Living on only four to five hours of sleep a night, reading voraciously, traveling to as many as three speeches in one day, constantly taking notes and meeting the public, Mead kept up the work habits she had taken on during the 1940s and 1950s, tack-

Eliminating World Hunger

In 1954, when Mead wrote this in her new preface to the Committee on Food Habits manual, Cultural Patterns and Technical Change, *the world had only begun to realize that whole countries could die of starvation—or be helped:*

"It is only very recently, actually only since World War II, that we have been able to share the hope that the peoples of the world need be hungry no longer.

But with the hope that misery can be prevented has come a new fear. . . . If the abolition of hunger and want were to be bought only by industrialization, by urbanization, by mechanization, by westernization, by secularization, by mass production, would not the cost be too great? . . .

Eyes light up at the vision that is offered. For the first time in history there is a possibility that no man need go well-fed to his rest, knowing that his neighbour is hungry, that indeed so many of his neighbours are hungry that though he broke the bread from his own table into a million pieces it would bring no real relief for a day, for an hour. But then faces fall, as people ask the second question: *How is it to be done*—in human terms? Granted that we know the technical answers: how to redistribute land in units which can support the use of modern agricultural machinery; how to locate industrial plants in relation to population and resources; how to utilize the local food supplies to provide a nutritional diet; how to reorganize town planning and water use so as to avoid the principal epidemic and endemic diseases in the world. Granted that we know all this, what will be the cost in terms of the human spirit? How much destruction of old values, disintegration of personality, alienation of parents from children, of husbands from wives, of students from teachers, of neighbour from neighbour, of the spirit of man from the faith and style of his traditional culture must there be? How slow must we go? How fast can we go?

ling more activities in a week than an ordinary person would think of attempting in a year. She had a devoted corps of secretaries, both at the museum and at Columbia University, and a following of graduate students whose careers were being advanced by their association with her. She could count on the secretaries of the organizations for which she worked to provide both a continual output of her speeches and a carefully planned calendar of activities including her involvement in the American Anthropological Association, the American Association for the Advancement of Science, the World Federation of Mental Health, the World Council of Churches, and the Institute of Intercultural Studies. To compensate for her lack of personal time, she counted on her friend, Rhoda Métraux, with whom she had shared an apartment since 1955, to take care of many of the daily details of her life.

An important media outlet opened up for Mead in 1961 when she began to write monthly columns for the women's magazine, *Redbook*. In *Redbook*, Margaret popularized many of the topics she had written about in her books, including: "School Prayers, Happiness and Telepathy" (February 1963), "What I Owe to Other Women" (April 1964), "A Cruise into the Past and a Glimpse of the Future" (February 1966), "Different Lands, Different Friendships"

(August 1966), "On Women" (August 1974), "Our Lives May Be at Stake" (November 1974), and "My First Marriage" (November 1972).

Her regular articles in *Redbook* called attention to her success as a woman and helped her to develop an understanding of women's role in society. Her ideas on education, sex roles, and mental health now began to mirror the goals of the women's liberation movement. While she was not in accord with all their positions, her example was an inspiration to thousands of women working for equal opportunity.

Besides her contributions to the popular media, her professional writing continued. She consistently wrote articles for the *American Anthropologist* and the World Federation of Mental Health journals, which were read by scientists and educators all over the world. Her views were respected because she was president of one or the other of the organizations during many of these years.

Mead speaks about housing for the poor before the American Association for the Advancement of Science.

Mead poses amongst exhibits in the Pacific Islands Hall at the Museum of Natural History.

Furthermore, many of Mead's books were reprinted several times to meet the demands of readers who learned about her through college classes, hearing her on the radio, going to one of her speeches, or reading her articles in such publications as *Redbook* and *Psychology Today*. Her books remained popular and were reprinted over and over.

Mead herself credited her wide acceptance to her anthropological know-how. But it was to her religious faith that she credited the strength she found to work so hard for the causes she believed in. She

was invited to work with the World Council of Churches. In accepting, she felt sure that her presence would be a force for tolerance and understanding among the religions of the world. Because she had studied ritual and belief in so many cultures, she served on an Episcopal church committee revising the *Book of Common Prayer* and was so faithful that she missed only one meeting in six years.

Helping the Cities

Many other projects interested Mead. As an anthropologist she had always noted that urbanization harmed cultures. Urbanized people, she believed, were hungrier and dirtier, died sooner, and had poorer educations and fewer rights. The 1960s brought poverty and unrest even in the United States. Mead now followed up her interest in people's housing and living conditions by accepting a special invitation to contribute to the science of human settlements (called *ekistics*) as part of the Delos Symposium. The Delos Symposium was a prestigious conference that annually called together thirty-five internationally respected authorities—for example, the reporter, Barbara Ward; the historian, Arnold Toynbee; and the inventor, Buckminster Fuller—to share their understanding of how cities worked and could be improved. Through her connection with the Delos Symposium, Mead began to advocate solutions to the complex problems of cities, such as poverty and discontent.

Mead's efforts to improve the conditions in cities caught on with Dr. Muriel Brown, a psychologist, who joined Mead in writing *The Wagon and the Star: A Study of American Community Initiative. The Wagon and the Star* shows how an individual citizen can make a real difference by seeing a problem, talking about it to neighbors, and helping to organize a group dedicated to solving it.

A Global Effort

Mead's writing became better known internationally. Her photographic study, *Family*, prepared in collaboration with photographer Ken Heyman and published in 1965, relies less on language than on visual images to emphasize all families' need for decent, private places in which to raise children. The photographs reveal the resilient spirits of families in the face of abject poverty.

In *Family*, Mead wrote:

> Most of the people, adults and children, photographed on the streets of strange cities, are poor. For it is prevailingly the poor of the world who gather on doorsteps, in parks, and on public beaches. They lack space indoors and have no gardens where their children can play safely under the trees. They lack walls to shut the stranger out of their lives. . . . As in our bodies we share our humanity, so also through the family we have a common heritage. This heritage provides us with a common language that survives and transcends all the differences . . . that divide [us]. And as [we] must now irrevocably perish or survive together, the task of each family is also the task of all humanity. This is to cherish the living, remember those who have gone before, and prepare for those who are not yet born.[66]

Mead stands before a blown-up illustration from her book, Family.

Mead was appointed to edit the report of the *President's Commission on Women*, which had been established by President John F. Kennedy in 1961 and was chaired by Eleanor Roosevelt. This report was published in 1965 and featured a thirty-page introduction by Mead, in which she summarized the progress made by women in achieving equal status. She reported that President Johnson had filled fifty-six posts with women by June of 1964 and that there were thirty-two State Commissions on the Status of Women. But more than jobs, Mead emphasized the importance of education in changing attitudes about

Adolescents Differ in Different Cultures

Mead never reversed her conclusions that culture provides most of the guidelines for the development of adolescents. In Family, *she speaks of developing an interest in art.*

"For many centuries civilizations have struggled with the problem of how to give men—and sometimes women—the freedom in which inspiration, knowledge, and art can flower. One solution has been to create a dichotomy in which the life of sex and parenthood has been set apart from a life of celibacy, asceticism, and thought or prayer. . . . [E]very child . . . had to choose between the pursuit of knowledge, on the one hand, and the life of the family, on the other. . . . In other societies, all boys have lived for a period apart from the secular world, as a way of giving them access to traditional knowledge. . . .

In most modern societies this selection and segregation of the few from the many is breaking down. However, . . . there is now developing in many parts of the modern world a new dichotomy based on sex. For increasingly, adolescent boys are being educated, while girls, like the vast majority of men and women in medieval Europe who chose parenthood, are asked to set aside their dreams of what they might become in favor of immediate marriage and parenthood.

In creating this new dichotomy we resemble the primitive peoples who did not understand paternity. For we do not take into account fatherhood or realize that in establishing a kind of society in which girls must become mothers as adolescents, before they have had time to become individuals, we also are forcing boys to become fathers before they have become individuals."

women. Educators and families, she said, had a responsibility to give girls the same opportunities as boys. Families would see the benefits in their daughters' feelings of increased self-worth:

The mother who can give her daughter confidence in her ability to understand mathematics will herself be more ready to use her own gifts in middle age. The father who is equally committed to his daughter's and to his son's education will find himself a less skeptical and a more sympathetic employer and colleague of women.[67]

Another national forum for Mead's work opened up when the Committee for Economic Development asked Mead to present a paper on "Equality Goals and Urban Progress." In this address, which she gave in 1966, just before the assassination of Dr. Martin Luther King Jr., she encouraged businesses to help change the environment in ghettos. Businesses could, she suggested, provide incentives that would attract the best professionals to fill important jobs in ghettos. Through a kind of quota system, businesses could give black workers a certain percentage of jobs. She advocated racial integration of all the professions, from medical doctors to poets, scientists, and musicians.

Back to the Field

In 1966, Mead was sixty-five years old and was full curator for the American Museum of Natural History. That year she and Rhoda Métraux went to New Guinea to update the museum's displays of Iatmul artifacts. She made two further trips to do restudies in New Guinea. In a letter written from Tambunam, New Guinea, she reveled in the beauty of the Sepik River:

> At last, on an early morning in June, 1967, I was on my way up the Sepik River, in New Guinea. More than four years had gone into the planning of this trip; and now, in a small speedboat, we raced up the seventy-mile stretch of river on the final stage of the trip, from the government station at Angoram to the village of Tambunam. The sun was just beginning to dissolve the banks of mist; on both shores the flat land stretched back, green and gold, as far

Students in Tambunam's new school, 1971. On her return trip to Tambunam, Mead found that the culture's child-rearing practices had become more nurturing.

> as the eye could see. Now we looked upon a new garden, with spirals of yam leaves climbing slender poles; now on a long bank of elephant grass, silver plumes bending to the breeze, now on a white heron, floating down to a dark beach. And on the river itself floating islands of grass, torn loose upriver, moved swiftly down stream with the current. The speedboat swerved around them, leaving a wide wake in the smooth brown water. Once we startled a crocodile—or was it only a waterlogged tree?[68]

In her powerful memory were the images of Tambunam as it had been, the proudest and handsomest village on the river, with great houses sixty feet long and thirty feet high ranged along the river bank . . . [when] . . . there were still men in Tambunam who wore the skin of the flying fox, permitted only to a man who had taken a head.[69]

No head-hunting or cannibalism had been reported since the chiefs had given up that practice. Mead saw that the pattern of adolescent life had changed primarily through a change in child-rearing practices. This had been the country in which Mead had felt so sympathetic toward the plight of little children, who were not treated tenderly. It had been the place where she had decided that she herself would be a parent and nurture her child.

Mead a Grandmother

The child that Margaret had decided to have was now married, and enjoyed an adult relationship with her mother. In 1969, a short time after Mead returned from her revisit to Tambunam, she became a grandmother. Catherine gave birth to a daughter, Sevanne Margaret. Margaret, characteristically, reflected on the anthropological dimensions of her new role. She said in her autobiography:

> As a new grandmother, I began both to relive my own daughter's infancy and to observe the manifestations of temperament in the tiny creature who was called Vanni—to note how she learned to ignore the noisy carpentry as the house was finished around her but was so sensitive to changes in the

human voice that her mother had to keep low background music playing to mask the change in tone of voice that took place when someone who had been speaking then answered the telephone. I remarked how she responded to pattern in the brightly colored chintzes and the mobiles that had been prepared for her.[70]

Shortly afterward, in 1969, Mead retired from the American Museum of Natural History with the title of curator emeritus. Retirement did not bring decreased activities, however. She became Chair of the Division of the Social Sciences at the

In 1969 Catherine (pictured here) gave birth to a daughter, Sevanne Margaret. Mead enjoyed her new role as a grandmother.

Mead (left) was inducted into the Women's Hall of Fame in 1965.

Jesuit school of higher education, Fordham University, in New York. As Chair, she helped start Fordham University's new inner-city Liberal Arts College at Lincoln Center, from 1968 to 1970.

During the 1960s Mead received many prizes and awards for her scientific achievements and world and civic service, which further enhanced and solidified her reputation. She was given the National Women Editors Award in 1965. Along with three other "outstanding women of the twentieth century," Mead was inducted into the Women's Hall of Fame in 1965. In 1969, she received the William Proctor Prize for Scientific Achievement from the Science Research Society of America.

Mead had experienced a long and extremely successful career. But despite her determination to participate in as many activities as she could, her health over the next few years would force her to slow down.

9 "Had We but World Enough, and Time"

—from a poem by Andrew Marvell (1621-1678), the inspiration for the title of Mead's last book, World Enough.

During the 1960s, Mead became involved in civil rights activities in the United States. As an anthropologist, she had always been tangentially involved in studies that tried to assess biological differences between races. Then in 1960, when Mead was president of the American Anthropological Association, the organization had asked the broader American Association for the Advancement of Science (AAAS) to do a study to see whether any new evidence had been found to prove blacks naturally inferior to whites. The study concluded that there was no evidence to prove that any race was naturally inferior in any way to any other.

Mead, as an influential member of the AAAS, convinced the organization to publicize their findings. Mead was part of a group of scientists who were disturbed that others were blaming the violent civil rights riots on blacks' supposed inferiority. Mead cooperated with Barry Commoner, an ecologist at Washington University, to plan an international meeting on the topic of the biological and social aspects of race. Mead and other editors then published a book of these meetings, called *Science and the Concept of Race.* As editor, Mead affirmed that no relationship existed between race and intelligence. Differences were cultural, she argued, and were caused by social conditions and education. Mead hoped that the book might alleviate racial tensions, but the violence continued. Dr. Martin Luther King Jr. and Robert F. Kennedy were assassinated in 1968. Two Black Panthers were murdered in Chicago. Mississippi police killed two black students at Jackson State University.

A Rap on Race

Because of Mead's involvement in *Science and the Concept of Race,* an unnamed media group working in the area of civil rights arranged for Mead to talk with the black writer, James Baldwin. For seven-and-a-half hours, on August 25-27, 1970, Mead and Baldwin recorded their conversation on race relations. It was published as *A Rap on Race.*

The two great leaders agreed on some issues—that the human race is one and that every person deserves equal opportunity. They also agreed on the injustice of slavery and that no one could give back what had been taken from black people.

But the harmony the media wished to achieve in these talks did not come about. Mead and Baldwin could not agree on the question of responsibility for the suffering of blacks. Mead held that she was not personally responsible for what had happened before she was born, and therefore did not share responsibility for the misery of blacks. Baldwin maintained that *all* whites had a responsibility to atone for slavery and the other wrongs done to blacks.

Mead could not see why she should make up or atone for wrongs that were done in the past, in history, when there was a future to hope for. She would not feel guilty over the past, she said, because that would keep her from working for the future. It was the present and the future for which she wished to take responsibility. To Baldwin, she said, "It could change your present if you could think of . . . a future where you would be at home."[71]

But Baldwin's feelings were too strong to permit him to forget the past. He answered,

During the 1960s Mead became an outspoken civil rights advocate.

We said responsibility is not guilt, did we not? I am not guilty of having sold myself onto that boat which got me here. You are not guilty of having starved out the Irish nation. But we are responsible.[72]

Baldwin also said that the assassination of Martin Luther King Jr. had ended hope for the future. He rejected Mead's focus on accepting his history "because it has brought nothing but death and misery to me and mine. . . . I intend to change it. How? I don't know yet. That is the question I live with. But the first step is to say no."[73] Although the two held different views, the talks were watched by thousands of people and solidified feelings on both sides.

More Return Trips to the Field

In the latter part of 1971, Mead and her friend, Rhoda Métraux, once again revisited Manus, Iatmul, Mundugumor, and Samoa, partly to see old friends, and partly to update the anthropological record on these cultures' preservation and progress. The two women spent a little time visiting the Arapesh, who had been resettled in a new village. Mead went to see the Iatmul at Tambunam, who still lived in houses built on stilts and stored their yams in dark houses with thatched, slanting roofs.

As Mead traveled, she was continually reminded of the lasting value of the anthropological work she had personally been involved in. In one mission, Don, a missionary-anthropologist, was using both Reo Fortune's analysis of the Arapesh language and Gregory Bateson's techniques

Rhoda Métraux (left) and Bill Mitchell (right) interview village men about a coming ceremony during a return trip to the Pacific Islands.

with films, stills, tapes, and notes. In what seemed to be a response to her UNESCO manual on food habits, the Arapesh had a trained nutritionist to help with the children.

At Peré Village Mead and Métraux visited the well-baby clinic, where the staff was inoculating infants and recording weights. They retraced Mead's 1932 trip up the Yuat River, in the East Sepik district, to the four Mundugumor villages. In her diary, Mead wrote about the changes she had seen, the pleasant and sad meetings with adults who had been children she studied in 1933:

> Afima is dead and Omblean is said to be senile. Yeshima and his brother came to call. Yeshima is a spry little old man, doesn't speak Pidgin. . . . A man came to say that he made the model crocodile for us in 1932.[74]

Omblean "had just had a stroke and needed to sit down on a stool. Even when he can't keep his attention on things, they

respect his position as a big man," she said.[75] She received the gift of an old hook and an old mask, the last things left of Alemi's old house, and promised to keep them safe in the museum.

When she visited a classroom, Mead noted that although the people had contributed many carvings to sell and raise funds, their money had been badly used. The schoolrooms still were not properly outfitted, and the teachers were very poorly prepared. The people seemed to have no say in how the mission was run or how religion was taught. But the children did enjoy reading and read a great deal.

On October 18 the two women celebrated Métraux's birthday, and the villagers celebrated the completion of a new house with a *naven* (new house) ceremony. The women waited in one house, the men in another. The anthropologists were ready with tape recorders and cameras, hoping they would see some of the old ways, and at dusk they were rewarded:

> The procession arrived, headed by the *wau*, the mother's brother, with his face blackened, dressed in green leaves and with a fringe of ferns around his face. The women wore grass skirts over their clothes. The *wau* danced in front, around and up into the house wearing a woman's big carrying bag, which he later gave to his wife to carry. This was just a teaser to stimulate the owner to buy a pig for the feast. I think teasers of this sort may have replaced the old trance sessions as a way of driving people into action.[76]

On the way back down the Yuat River in a speedboat, Mead remembered her 1932 trip, which had taken two days by canoe. Downriver she and Métraux parted,

Métraux to photograph Iatmul ceremonials and Mead to continue home alone.

When she arrived again in the United States, she had more awards to accept: the 1971 Arches of Science Award, given by the Pacific Science Center for her work with Oceanic cultures; the 1971 Joseph Priestley Award, given by Dickinson College to encourage young anthropologists; and the 1971 Kalinga Prize for the Popularization of Science, given by UNESCO and the government of India. She was also asked to co-chair the United States Task Force on the Future of Mankind, and the Role of the Churches in a World of Science-based Technology, for the World Council of Churches.

In 1973, at seventy-two, Mead returned again to Peré to document the continuing changes, but with less energy than before. In a letter written on July 23, 1973, she commented:

> I am alone in the village, the first time I have been alone in a New Guinea village since 1966, when I spent many weeks here while the people were completely absorbed in preparing for the big Christmas that was to celebrate the merging of the old South Coast Council, which Paliau had started, with the new one. Everyone was exhausted in the evenings and preoccupied in the daytime. My lamp used to go out and I would rebel at the wasted time or try to read in bed with a flashlight. This year we have been going to bed early and often I have lain awake for hours, but somehow no longer rebelling, just thinking. Occasionally I turn on the flashlight and make a note of something that seems worth catching. But I am getting enough sleep, keeping up with each day's work, buffered against the welter of decisions and dilemmas which will crowd in as soon as I get back to New York. Four to five hours a day is about all I can do well on a stiff manual typewriter. Then I begin to put the carbons in backwards or make too many typos.[77]

Two years later, in 1975, she made yet another trip to Manus. The village was still

Peré canoe on way to market, 1975. On her third visit to Peré, Mead found that the village was still undergoing many changes.

Peré Village Three, 1975

In her Letters from the Field *of July 23, 1975, Mead describes her visit to the Manus village, which had been remapped the third time.*

"It is a quiet village. Not once have we heard angry shouting voices, fighting cocks, fighting dogs, beleaguered squealing pigs. At high tide the moored canoes bump gently against each other and the thatch rustles and crackles. Every morning a procession of roosters appear on the square and crow in concert without conflict. The people are scattered again, each household secure within the space allotted for its own clan, each clan with a piece of beach where canoes can be seared with torches, outriggers mended, nets dried without the contentiousness that used to occur over the wharf in New Peré One, when the village plan had been based on social standing and officialdom rather than on kinship. Then when the village treasurers were unable to resist the importunities [begging] of their kin and the funds entrusted to their keeping dwindled and disappeared, the money was divided among the clans. Each clan was made the custodian of its own funds, responsible for its own share.

Later, when New Peré Three was designed, the clan formation was restored, with Patusi—the village that moved in and swamped New Peré Two—at the far end with a small adequate square of its own. Later still the custom grew up of each clan having one or more canteens—a small trade store that keeps tobacco, canned meat, canned fish, batteries, cookies, etc. Trade stores come to grief in New Guinea because the storekeeper gives too much credit to his kin and eventually the store goes bankrupt. Now a group of kin invest in a canteen and if they borrow it blind, there is no great harm done as they are merely recouping their investment. And actual borrowing is reduced because there is a store where things can be bought."

changing. Now the Manus Usiai people from the island's interior had come to live at Peré Village on the shore. With characteristic generosity, she spoke with Nahau, a leader of the Usiai, and helped her write a ten-page paper for her and other young people, giving advice on how to construct a constitution for the emerging country, now called Papua New Guinea.

From 1973 to 1976 Mead worked with the United Nations. She contributed to the United Nations Mission Statement and attended the United Nations World Conference on Population in Stockholm as a guest. She "was involved with the beginning of Earth Day and the notion of ringing the United Nations Peace Bell at the moment of the spring solstice."[78] In 1976 she participated in Habitat, the United Nations Conference on Human Settlements, in Vancouver, Canada.

Mead continued to write, working with Ken Heyman on their second book of world commentary and photographs. He had gone around the world to document the process of aging. Together Mead and Heyman analyzed the pictures, and Mead wrote the text for their new book, *World Enough: Rethinking the Future* (1975). In the introduction, she told how they had first listed their ideas when Heyman had come to her with his project to "do a book about the world." She had thought:

> Perhaps, if we could show the same people over a span of years—children grown to adulthood, hands gnarled with heavy work, women's once uplifted breasts sagging from having nursed many children, tractors succeeding oxen in the fields, pumps for the wells where women once drew water—we would be able to bring to life, for the inhabitants of the last quarter of the twentieth century, the changes that were going on in the world.[79]

In *World Enough*, Mead said that people need to start creating an open society and make the world one in which each person treats all others as members of the same human race.

Winding Down

Mead did not begin to slow down until 1978, when physical pain, deafness, and weakness began to affect her. She refused to believe the doctors who told her she had pancreatic cancer. She kept working hard, scheduling trips and speeches into the 1980s. Only a few people knew in the summer of 1978 that she was really ill. She continued to write her regular columns for *Redbook*, the last one of which appeared after her death. Only when she had to go to the hospital did she cancel her appointments and travel. Even while she was dying she spoke about her plans for the world. Her death from cancer

Mead addresses the National Women's Conference in 1977. Despite serious illness, Mead continued to schedule trips and speeches into the 1980s.

Mead Compares Real Life and Anthropology

Anthropological work is really a part of life, Mead says in her Letter *from Mundugumor in October 1971.*

"For a people whose lives are bounded within a few square miles and whose relationships are confined to a few hundred men and women and children, every birth, every death, every marriage and every quarrel carries a tremendous burden of meaning. Every event is described again and again. Only in this way will the children learn what life is and how it is to be lived. . . .

Meanwhile, on the other side of the world, I too had relived the same moments—felt the same horror at the idea of a baby born with a tail, recalled the wetness of the rainy night at Kangleme during the crocodile hunt. All these experiences came back to me again and again as I wrote and lectured and analyzed films and photographs, extracting from each intensely observed and recorded event some meaning for the wider understanding of human culture. Although the framework appears to be so different (a primitive village of recent headhunters and a lecture room at Columbia University), there is a matching of intensity in my observation and in the Tambunam attentiveness to each detail."

came on November 15, 1978.

There were nine national memorial services in her honor. The largest of the nine was held at the American Museum of Natural History memorial on January 20, 1979. Andrew Young, then U.S. ambassador to the United Nations, presented her daughter, Catherine, with the Presidential Medal of Freedom in Mead's honor. One after another, the scientists and politicians and friends and acquaintances stood up to honor her memory, to describe her greatest strengths, or to give

her credit for a kindness, an inspiration, a clue to an anthropological mystery. Mead's biographer, Jane Howard, who was present, tells how Buckminster Fuller, her friend from the Delos Symposium days,

famous for talking on and on, was, for a change, remarkably laconic. "I know she can hear me," he explained when his turn came to speak. Then, looking upward, he added, "We love you, Margaret."[80]

The New Climate of Opinion

Four years after Mead's death, her reputation and lasting importance were tested. On January 31, 1983, the *New York Times* ran a sensational three-page story about a forthcoming book by the Australian anthropologist, Derek Freeman. In his book, *Margaret Mead and Samoa: The Making and Unmaking of an Anthropological Myth,* Freeman claimed to discredit Mead's Samoan research. His own field work in western Samoa did give a different picture of Samoa than Mead's. Before the end of the year, twenty-four national newspapers and magazines had followed up on what seemed a national scandal.

Ten years later, in 1993, the disagreement between Mead's and Freeman's approaches are still being discussed in *American Anthropologist.* Young and old scientists who knew and worked with Mead have reexamined their field and her contributions. In general, Freeman and Mead used very different approaches. Freeman criticized Mead's use of adolescent girls as her sources, claiming that his own adult male authority figures were more reliable. Anthropologists today believe that either approach results in an incomplete picture of a culture, but that Freeman's sources were slightly less valid than Mead's. Freeman also criticized the informality of Mead's notes. But Freeman's notes were so scien-

tific as to be impossible for lay people to read.

So, ten years later Mead's worth was proven in just the way she would have liked. The difference between her picture of Samoa and Freeman's turns out to be the difference between looking to women

Mead, a pioneer in the field of anthropology, had a major influence on the way we look at humanity.

Attitudes Toward Childbearing

In World Enough: Rethinking the Future, *Mead reiterates her high value for the unique power of a woman to bear a human child.*

"The need to bear many children so that a few will survive is being replaced by the admonition to bear fewer children because those who are born will live.

We can see all these changes as freeing both men and women from the burdens of parenthood, as societies in the past have been willing to do when they perceived that their population was growing too fast. Where once we had the voluntary celibacy of the monk and nun, the mendicant, the armies who wandered from land to land, the men who left home when their first child was born, we now have artificial methods which separate sexual intercourse from procreation. Today, the bodies of women are changing from something natural, to which men and women had to submit, into something like a machine whose timing and activities can be deliberately controlled."

or to men as the source of information. Mead based her book on female adolescent informants and all her projects were centered on women and children and their interests and points of view. Freeman based his studies on information collected from adult male authority figures, and his projects center on men's interests and concerns. It is somehow fitting that the lasting worth of Mead's work centered on women.

Mead was concerned with the way women, children, and adolescents in every society are treated and how they live.

Freeman's attack did not destroy Mead's reputation. Rather, both the public and the anthropologists renewed their efforts to learn and discuss more. Anthropologists rededicated themselves to the values of their field, the controversy merely reminding the world that science always expects new information to be brought forward.

In his review of the Freeman book, James Clifford compares Mead's and Freeman's differing visions of field work and ethnography. He considers them both old fashioned compared to what anthropology has now been called upon to do—to provide a "two-directional journey examining the realities of both sides of cultural differences so that they may mutually question each other."[81] What else did Mead ask for but this? he wonders. That was her goal—a climate in which women and men, children and adults, scientists and laborers, writers and football players, artists and carpenters each have an equal opportunity to be a person. Clifford reflects that Mead's

> influential books helped Americans see that American adolescent patterns of rebelliousness and American sex roles were not "natural," but culturally molded, and so might be altered through different child-rearing methods. Such cultural criticism of America worked by juxtaposing alternative patterns elsewhere in the world: that is, real world examples, not utopian fantasies. In today's more sophisticated world we know that the Samoan and New Guinea societies are more complicated than Margaret Mead described, as also is America.[82]

These anthropologists' favorable opinions have been reflected in even more recent surveys. In their Fall 1990 special issue, *Life* magazine named Mead one of "The 100 Most Important Americans of the Twentieth Century." She was among thirteen women named after the magazine interviewed nearly 100 consultants. In March 1993, the National Women's Hall of Fame and the Siena Research Institute honored "The Most Influential Women of the Twentieth Century." Mead was named among the top five.

What did Margaret work for? Why did she speak and write, except to contribute to our knowledge of human beings? She herself did so by searching, haranguing, questioning, observing, probing, photographing, recording, reading, and contradicting. And "that," said her daughter Catherine in response to Freeman, "is called science."[83] The argument, the airing of issues, the open exchange of ideas—

that, she said, is called a favorable climate of opinion.

Mead would have been the first to admit that science needed to be constantly updated and changed, as her recurring visits to the field attested. In the end, Mead stands as a pioneer and a full participant in a worldwide movement for equality and understanding.

As Mead's biographer, Robert Cassidy, writes:

> Margaret Mead's attitudes about race and social justice were shaped at an early age. As a young girl, she was reminded that her paternal grandfather, Giles F. Mead, had fought on the Union side in the Civil War; and when Margaret was ten years old the family moved to a Bucks County farmhouse that had been a station in the Underground Railroad. Her mother taught young Margaret to call the Negro woman who worked for them "Mrs." and instilled in her the necessity to show "tremendous care" for the poor and anyone who was different. It was her mother who opened young Margaret's eyes to the stark realities of racial abuse, when she informed the eleven-year-old girl that the wife of one of the ex-slaves living in town had been raped by a white man and that was why she had a half-white son. And it was Emily Fogg Mead who, through her own field of study of conditions among Italian-American immigrants . . . impressed upon Margaret the need for optimism in relations with those less fortunate.[84]

Notes

Chapter 1: An Unconventional Childhood

1. Margaret Mead, *Blackberry Winter: My Earlier Years.* New York: William Morrow, 1972.
2. Mead, *Blackberry Winter.*
3. Mead, *Blackberry Winter.*
4. Mead, *Blackberry Winter.*
5. Mead, *Blackberry Winter.*
6. Mead, *Blackberry Winter.*
7. Mead, *Blackberry Winter.*
8. Mead, *Blackberry Winter.*
9. Mead, *Blackberry Winter.*
10. Mead, *Blackberry Winter.*
11. Mead, *Blackberry Winter.*

Chapter 2: College and Career—Meeting the Right People

12. Mead, *Blackberry Winter.*
13. Mead, *Blackberry Winter.*
14. Jane Howard, *Margaret Mead: A Life.* New York: Simon & Schuster, 1984.
15. Mead, *Blackberry Winter.*
16. Mead, *Blackberry Winter.*

Chapter 3: Six Months in Samoa

17. Margaret Mead, *Letters from the Field 1925-1975.* New York: Harper & Row, 1977.
18. Margaret Mead, *Coming of Age in Samoa: A Psychological Study of Primitive Youth for Western Civilization.* New York: William Morrow, 1961.
19. Mead, *Coming of Age in Samoa.*
20. Mead, *Blackberry Winter.*
21. Margaret Mead, *Ruth Benedict.* New York: Columbia University Press, 1974.
22. Howard, *Margaret Mead: A Life.*
23. Mead, *Blackberry Winter.*

Chapter 4: Working with Five More Cultures

24. Mead, *Letters from the Field.*
25. Mead, *Letters from the Field.*
26. Mead, *Letters from the Field.*
27. Mead, *Letters from the Field.*
28. Mead, *Blackberry Winter.*
29. Margaret Mead, *Growing Up in New Guinea: A Comparative Study of Primitive Education.* New York: William Morrow, 1962.
30. Mead, *Growing Up in New Guinea.*
31. Mead, *Growing Up in New Guinea.*
32. Mead, *Letters from the Field.*
33. Mead, *Letters from the Field.*
34. Mead, *Letters from the Field.*
35. Mead, *Blackberry Winter.*
36. Mead, *Blackberry Winter.*
37. Mead, *Blackberry Winter.*
38. Mead, *Blackberry Winter.*

Chapter 5: Beautiful Bali with Gregory Bateson

39. Audio-Text Cassettes, "The State of the Sexes."
40. Mead, *Blackberry Winter.*
41. Mead, *Letters from the Field.*
42. Mead, *Blackberry Winter.*
43. Mead, *Letters from the Field.*
44. Mead, *Blackberry Winter.*
45. Robert Cassidy, *Margaret Mead: A Voice for the Century.* New York: Universe Books, 1982.

Chapter 6: Motherhood and Wartime Anthropology

46. Mead, *Blackberry Winter.*
47. Mead, *Blackberry Winter.*
48. Mead, *Blackberry Winter.*

49. Mead, *Blackberry Winter*.

50. Mead, *Blackberry Winter*.

51. Mead, *Blackberry Winter*.

52. Mead, *Blackberry Winter*.

53. Margaret Mead, *And Keep Your Powder Dry*. New York: William Morrow, 1942.

54. Howard, *Margaret Mead: A Life*.

55. Mead, *Blackberry Winter*.

Chapter 7: Ambassador-at-Large, 1945-1953

56. Margaret Mead, *Cultural Patterns and Technical Change*. New York: UNESCO, 1955.

57. Mary Catherine Bateson, *With a Daughter's Eye: A Memoir of Margaret Mead and Gregory Bateson*. New York: William Morrow, 1984.

58. Bateson, *With a Daughter's Eye*.

59. Howard, *Margaret Mead: A Life*.

60. Mead, *Letters from the Field*.

61. Mead, *Letters from the Field*.

62. Mead, *Letters from the Field*.

63. Mead, *Letters from the Field*.

Chapter 8: Museum Work and Increasing Recognition

64. Bateson, *With a Daughter's Eye*.

65. Mead, *Blackberry Winter*.

66. Margaret Mead with Ken Heyman, *Family*. New York: Macmillan, 1965.

67. Margaret Mead, ed., and Frances Bagley Kaplan, *American Women: The Report of the President's Commission on the Status of Women and Other Publications of the Commission*. New York: Charles Scribner's Sons, 1965.

68. Mead, *Letters from the Field*.

69. Mead, *Letters from the Field*.

70. Mead, *Blackberry Winter*.

Chapter 9: "Had We but World Enough, and Time"

71. Margaret Mead and James Baldwin, *A Rap on Race*. Philadelphia: J. B. Lippincott, 1971.

72. Mead and Baldwin, *A Rap on Race*.

73. Mead and Baldwin, *A Rap on Race*.

74. Mead, *Letters from the Field*.

75. Mead, *Letters from the Field*.

76. Mead, *Letters from the Field*.

77. Mead, *Letters from the Field*.

78. Bateson, *With a Daughter's Eye*.

79. Margaret Mead, *World Enough: Rethinking the Future*. Boston: Little, Brown, 1975.

80. Howard, *Margaret Mead: A Life*.

Epilogue: The New Climate of Opinion

81. James Clifford and George E. Marcus, eds., *Writing Culture: The Poetics and Politics of Ethnography*. Berkeley: University of California Press, 1986.

82. Clifford and Marcus, eds., *Writing Culture: The Poetics and Politics of Ethnography*.

83. Howard, *Margaret Mead: A Life*.

84. Cassidy, *Margaret Mead: A Voice for the Century*.

For Further Reading

Books and articles by Mead

Margaret Mead, *Anthropologists and What They Do.* New York: Watts, 1965.

—————————, *Coming of Age in Samoa: A Psychological Study of Primitive Youth for Western Civilization.* New York: William Morrow & Company, 1961. Mead's best-selling book about her first field trip.

—————————, *Growing Up in New Guinea: A Comparative Study of Primitive Education.* New York: William Morrow & Company, 1968. Written in the same style as her first best-seller; about her Manus field trip. Contains reflections on Samoa and the United States.

—————————, "Image of the Scientist Among High School Students: A Pilot Study" (with Rhoda Métraux), *Science,* vol. 126 (August 30, 1937), pp. 384-90. Study for teachers and educators in a popular style.

—————————, "I've Always Been a Woman . . . I've Never Been an Imitation Man" (with Joan Wixen), *The Sunday News Magazine,* Detroit, June 22, 1975. Lively conversation when Mead is seventy-four years old.

—————————, *An Interview with Santa Claus.* New York: Walker, 1978. A children's story, reprinted from *Redbook,* in which Mead retells many cultural and historical tales about Santa Claus.

—————————, *Letters from the Field 1925-1975* (planned and edited by Ruth Nanda Anshen). New York: Harper & Row, 1977. A cross section of Mead's correspondence from Samoa and New Guinea, selected from the complete collection at the Huntington Library.

—————————, "Man on the Moon," from *Some Personal Views,* ed. by Rhoda Métraux. New York: Walker, 1979. This book is a collection of a large number of Mead's *Redbook* articles.

Audio-Text Cassettes

These and many other tapes record Mead's speeches and comments.

Milton Eisenhower, Margaret Mead, and Robert Ardrey, "The American Character: Violent America." N. Hollywood, CA: Center for Cassette Studies, recording #25884. The three distinguished social scientists discuss the tremendous increase in both individual and collective violence.

Margaret Mead, "The Women's Revolution. The State of the Sexes." N. Hollywood, CA: Center for Cassette Studies, recording #35040. Mead reviews the evolution of social roles and gives her position on laws regarding the use of marijuana.

Margaret Mead and James Mitchell, "Perspectives in Anthropology. The World of Margaret Mead." N. Hollywood, CA:Center for Cassette Studies, recording #010/3105. Mead discusses social structures with Mitchell, a young anthropologist.

Books about Mead

Mary Catherine Bateson, *With a Daughter's Eye: A Memoir of Margaret Mead and Gre-*

gory Bateson. New York: William Morrow, 1984. Mead's daughter tells about her relationships with her parents.

Robert Cassidy, *Margaret Mead: A Voice for the Century.* New York: Universe Books, 1982. A synopsis of Mead's most famous theories and accomplishments. Arranged by topic

Jane Howard, *Margaret Mead: A Life.* New York: Simon & Schuster, 1984. A com-plete biography with a balanced approach. Howard did many personal interviews with people who knew Mead.

Lowell Holmes, *Samoan Village: Case Studies in Cultural Anthropology* (general editors, George and Louise Spindler). New York: Holt, Rinehart, & Winston, 1974. Assesses Mead's work in Samoa.

Works Consulted

Margaret Mead, *And Keep Your Powder Dry*. New York: William Morrow, 1975. Readable summary of Mead's view of Americans during World War II and her opinion on how they could improve America.

——————, *Balinese Character: A Photographic Analysis* (with Gregory Bateson; edited by Wilbur G. Valentine). Special Publications, vol. 2. New York: New York Academy of Sciences, 1942. Difficult reading but wonderful pictures of the Balinese people.

——————, *Cultural Patterns and Technical Change*. New York: UNESCO, 1955. Gives a postwar perspective on economic recovery and U.S. policy.

——————, *Family* (with Ken Heyman). New York: Macmillan, 1965. Pictures of families from many countries, with Mead's cultural analysis and ideas on education and policy.

——————, *Male and Female: A Study of the Sexes in a Changing World*. New York: William Morrow, 1975. Further analysis of temperament and how culture affects the way men and women perceive their roles.

——————, *New Lives for Old: Cultural Transformation—Manus, 1928-1953*. New York: Dell, 1968. Mead's restudy of the Manus after they gave up their old ways.

——————, *A Rap on Race* (with James Baldwin). Philadelphia: J.B. Lippincott, 1971. Transcript of the seven-and-a-half-hour conversation between Mead and Baldwin.

——————, *Ruth Benedict*. New York: Columbia University Press, 1974. Mead's biography of her long-time friend.

——————, *The School in American Culture: The Inglis Lecture for 1950*. Cambridge, MA: Harvard University Press, 1971. Mead's mid-century ideas on how to improve education in the United States.

——————, *Sex and Temperament in Three Primitive Societies*. New York: Dell, 1971. Mead's most complete discussion of the Arapesh, Mundugumor, and Tchambuli cultures as she saw their men and women interacting in the education of their children.

——————, *World Enough: Rethinking the Future* (photographs by Ken Heyman). Boston: Little, Brown, 1975. Long chapters review all Mead's anthropological, environmental, and educational concerns. Beautiful pictures of aged and young people from many lands.

Margaret Mead, ed., and Frances Bagley Kaplan, *American Women: The Report of the President's Commission on the Status of Women and Other Publications of the Commission*. New York: Charles Scribner's Sons, 1965. Mead summarizes the state of women in U.S. society after the commission completed its study.

Index

Credits

About the Author

Rafael Tilton is an educator, editor and writer who has written two other books for young people. Rafael Tilton's fascination for cultural traditions began with reading folklore and mythology as a grade school student. After meeting and discussing cultures with friends who were students of anthropology, Tilton found a new interest in the scientific techniques needed by field workers. Tilton's volunteer work involving single mothers and their children brought a personal dimension to this study of the famous woman anthropologist, Margaret Mead.